"What a great book! It's filled with so much valuable information that, although it's divided into weekly sections, you'll be tempted to read the whole book at once. You won't want to wait for next week's installment. Whether you want to repair a broken marriage or revitalize a fairly solid one, this book will lead the way."

Michele Weiner-Davis
www.divorcebusting.com
Author of *Divorce Busting*

"We all need skills to chart an easier course in our marriage relationships. Chuck provides these coaching resources by giving real-life stories and concrete methods to help maneuver through relationship challenges. If your relationship is stagnant and needs a re-boot or is good, but you want to make it better, I recommend this book. You and your marriage are worth the weekly focus provided."

Stephen Arterburn
Founder and Chairman of New Life Ministries
Host of Christian radio talk show
New Life Live! and best-selling Author

"*Marriage Recall* is an exquisite book! Throughout this much-needed compilation, my friend and colleague Chuck Fallon deftly equips couples with practical tools and essential skills which will help marriages thrive. I knew *Marriage Recall* was a winner when I emailed my wife entire sections, asking that we read them together."

Michael John Cusick
Counselor, Speaker and Author of *Surfing for God*

"I consider Chuck a good friend on the journey of life. His wit and depth have brightened my soul and will be sure to brighten yours as well."

Ben Wilson
Founder, Marriages Restored
Licensed Professional Counselor

"Chuck Fallon has a solid grip on proven principals for a great marriage, and at the same time offers lighthearted and refreshing counsel. According to Chuck, "the secret of marriage is... there is no secret!" What does exist are dozens and dozens of golden nuggets that will lift your spirits and carry you toward that golden wedding band of success."

Jim Walters
Senior Pastor, Bear Valley Church
Author of *When Faith Takes Flight*

"*Marriage Recall* is insightful, funny, engaging and very practical. Read this book as a couple to measure where you are now and how you can move toward a more engaged and fulfilling married life. Like the book says, "You can do this!" This book is chock-full of practical resources and working examples."

Frank Walker, MA
Author, Marriage Counselor
Chapel Grace, Coalinga, CA

MARRIAGE
RECALL

MARRIAGE
RECALL

REMEMBER • REPAIR • RELOVE

52 WEEKLY REMINDERS ON
HOW TO LOVE DURING
THE EVERYDAY OF LIFE

CHUCK FALLON, LPC

MARRIAGE RECALL

Published by ScriptArt, LLC
P.O. Box 150334, Lakewood, Colorado 80215

ISBN: 978-0-9892782-0-1

Cover, Book Design and Editing: ScriptArt, Jan Fallon
Tin Can Phones Illustration © 2013 Jan Fallon

Printed in the United States of America

To my dear friend and mentor, Charlie Turnbo

Our time together was far too short, but your authentic faith in Jesus and words of wisdom to me have changed the course of my life.

Thank you.

ACKNOWLEDGMENTS

Jesus—for giving me new life, filled with purpose and hope. I long to know you better.

Jan—for loving God, taking a risk on a blind date, and daring to believe our journey matters! Thank you for the creative devotion you gave to the design and content of this work.

Jerry, Gabe, and Micah—for teaching me about a heavenly Father's love as I experience loving you. Many of my dreams are inspired because I want to share with you the richness of this gift called life. I believe in you.

Michele Weiner-Davis and the Divorce Busting team—for letting me get into the trenches with so many hurting people fighting for their marriages. I learn so much from you.

Steve Arterburn, Sharon Barnes, Jim Phillis and the New Life team—for your dedication to helping so many. Thank you for including me.

Michael Cusick, Ben and Ann Wilson—for the honesty of your stories and the contagious way you invite me to wrestle with my own.

Jim Walters and David Rupert—for supplying the brotherly nudge that encouraged me as this book took shape.

So many courageous clients—for fighting for what matters. You are an inspiration to me, and to those who will read this book.

CONTENTS

ACKNOWLEDGMENTS...8
INTRODUCTION...11

SECTION ONE - REMEMBER 13

WEEK 1 - BE INTENTIONAL 15
WEEK 2 - COMPLAIN WITHOUT BLAME............................19
WEEK 3 - BATTLESHIP 23
WEEK 4 - WHAT DO YOU EXPECT?...................................27
WEEK 5 - UNLOAD 31
WEEK 6 - DEFINING FORGIVENESS...................................35
WEEK 7 - DIG A LITTLE DEEPER 39
WEEK 8 - DON'T DRIBBLE THE FOOTBALL 43
WEEK 9 - RESPECTING THE WALL......................................47
WEEK 10 - WHERE'S YOUR HEART?...................................51
WEEK 11 - TRANSFORMATION..55
WEEK 12 - TURN AROUND 59
WEEK 13 - MR. NICE GUY...63
WEEK 14 - DO NOT RUN! 67
WEEK 15 - LAUGH 71
WEEK 16 - ME OVERREACT? NEVER! 75
WEEK 17 - CAPICHE?..79
WEEK 18 - DEAFENING SILENCE 83
WEEK 19 - DON'T BLAME ME!..87
WEEK 20 - MINDREADING (IS) FOR DUMMIES 91
WEEK 21 - HOW TO BE NAKED IN MARRIAGE 95
WEEK 22 - DISAGREE (WITHOUT BEING DISAGREEABLE).....99
WEEK 23 - OH NO! I'M HUNGRY! 103
WEEK 24 - THIS IS MY EXIT 107

SECTION TWO - REPAIR 111

WEEK 25 - FOCUS ON THE VALUE 113

WEEK 26 - IDENTIFY THE TEST.....................................117

WEEK 27 - PASSING THE TEST.......................................121

WEEK 28 - RESPECT YOURSELF!....................................125

WEEK 29 - COMING ALIVE! 129

WEEK 30 - THE OPPOSITE ATTRACTION 133

WEEK 31 - THE GOOD STUFF..137

WEEK 32 - THE HUNT 141

WEEK 33 - DISQUALIFIERS...145

WEEK 34 - GETTING PAID..149

WEEK 35 - WRONG FOOT 153

WEEK 36 - THOSE WE DO NOT SPEAK OF 157

WEEK 37 - DON'T SAY IT, DO IT! 161

WEEK 38 - ASK ME AGAIN! 165

WEEK 39 - YAY FOR THE 10K! 169

WEEK 40 - DON'T GIVE UP 173

WEEK 41 - BETWEEN MAGICAL AND MISERABLE 177

WEEK 42 - OKAY, GIVE UP!..181

WEEK 43 - DROP THE ROPE 185

WEEK 44 - MOLEHILLS OUT OF MOUNTAINS...............189

WEEK 45 - THE RED HERRING 193

WEEK 46 - OVERCOME THE ODDS 197

WEEK 47 - THAT IS THE QUESTION...............................201

SECTION THREE - RELOVE 205

RELOVE INTRODUCTION...207

WEEK 48 - BOOKS TO READ 208

WEEK 49 - AUDIO/VIDEO TO ENJOY 209

WEEK 50 - SURVEYS TO TAKE 210

WEEK 51 - SITES TO SURF 211

WEEK 52 - PLACES TO GO 212

TIN CAN PHONES 213
CONTACT CHUCK 214

INTRODUCTION

Marriage Recall is a compilation of 52 weekly reminders on *how to love* during the *everyday* of life. It's a welcome knowledge-base to help keep your marriage on track or a trusty handbook on how to navigate through the tougher seasons—no matter how long you've been married.

It can be used by couples, individuals, or in small groups. The chapters are short and filled with practical advice and humor, covering a specific skill or perspective—with a weekly journal page so you can apply it to your own situation. Read them in any order you would like.

The steps are doable, even simple—but they are not *easy*! They rub against what has become *standard practice* in your marriage. They ask you to do something *different*, if you are in a rut. They invite you to change something that seems insignificant, but *truly isn't*—so that the displaced value of your marriage can be *remembered* and *repaired*.

Section One—Remember, focuses on how to build communication skills and resolve conflict. Section Two—Repair, offers techniques to help with tough issues like infidelity, separation, or divorce. Section Three—Relove, suggests resources to enhance your marriage that often go ignored until getting help is critical.

It's my suggestion that you read the entire book. If you do, you'll be ready to help yourself, your spouse, and other couples be *intentional* about building a successful marriage.

You can do this!

SECTION ONE - REMEMBER

REMEMBER • REPAIR • RELOVE

REMEMBER • REPAIR • RELOVE

WEEK 1 - BE INTENTIONAL

Friends of mine took a couple out for dinner for their 50th wedding anniversary. This older couple was so full of love. He stood tall as he opened the door for her. Her eyes twinkled with delight as she looked at him. My friend commented, "You must have been so in love when you got married for it to last this long!" The couple giggled knowingly as they shared their secret—they met on their wedding day. Their marriage was arranged! It was the decisions they made *after* they married that nurtured their love for five decades.

I asked students in a marriage class I taught to interview a couple that had been successfully married for at least twenty-five years. This is one of my favorite assignments! One interview question asked, "How did you make it through the difficult times?" Paper after paper listed difficult experiences, such as financial failure, the loss of a child, health problems, and infidelity. There wasn't a "one-size-fits-all" answer to how the couples worked through their challenges. The point is they found a way.

These two stories have a very consistent message. Thriving marriages are intentional—they don't just happen. They are nurtured, studied, cultivated, maintained, and repaired. They are cared for.

If the grass is greener on the other side of the fence it's because the neighbors are taking better care of their grass! When it comes to growing your marriage, you can complain about it, or you can learn the basics to make it better.

When my bride came down the aisle on our wedding day, her entrance song included these words:

It's not the morning
Not the easy times that have proven my heart
It's when I see that the darkness can't tear us apart
(*After The Sunset* by Debbie McNeil)

We didn't know what darkness would come, but we married for better or worse, through sickness and in health, for richer or poorer. When darkness comes, we know we'll go through it together, it can't tear us apart.

Here's the secret to a thriving marriage—there is no secret! Learn the basics, practice them until you are exceptionally good at loving your spouse, and then practice them some more. If something doesn't work, give it more time. If it's still not productive, try a different path. Don't let the darkness tear you apart. Find a way. Be intentional.

The steps I've written about for a thriving marriage aren't magical; they're not simple; they're not easy. They're hard work. But they've been rewarding to many of my clients. I hope you find inspiration, hope, and encouragement to intentionally invest in your marriage.

You can do this!

MARRIAGE RECALL

Mark what impact this topic is currently having on your marriage:

1	2	③	4	5

none   **needs reminder**   **needs repair**

Describe a similar experience you had relating with your spouse:

_____

_____

_____

What can you do differently using the skill outlined in this chapter?

_____

_____

_____

This week, apply your new skill and record your experience:

_____

_____

_____

_____

_____

_____

_____

Make a new mark to track your progress. Don't give up!

1	2	3	4	5

none   **needs reminder**   **needs repair**

REMEMBER • REPAIR • RELOVE

WEEK 2 - COMPLAIN WITHOUT BLAME

I read some research a while ago that was not at all surprising. It determined that couples who have little or no conflict in the first year of marriage report being happier. However, if they have not had at least a moderate level of conflict to resolve by year three, the same couples report feeling less connected and less secure in their marriages.

This indicates that conflict is needed to secure a healthy bond with your spouse.

The presence of conflict doesn't guarantee a healthy marriage. It's important to learn conflict resolution skills. How conflict begins can determine whether it will be resolved successfully. I encourage you to learn what marriage expert Dr. John Gottman calls the soft start-up using the acronym DEAR.

Describe the situation in a factual and neutral way. "Yesterday when I picked out those sunglasses for you at the store, you immediately turned your back to me, and modeled them for our friends."

Express your feelings using "I" statements without passing blame. "I was stunned and hurt. I know you didn't mean anything by it, but you know that I sometimes feel invisible. When you turned away from me, I was surprised how sharp it felt." If you're the listener, allow yourself to be curious about what you're hearing as your spouse moves to the next step.

Assert what you want. "I wish you had shown the glasses to me first, before showing our friends. Can you include me next time?" This sounds obvious, but it's more difficult than it seems. Communication is goal-oriented. You want something every time you communicate. It may be acknowledgment, an apology, or a hug. It could be something deeper that you're not aware of until you verbally explore your complaint. When you assert what you want, you have a higher chance of getting what you need.

Repeat as needed. This process can take some practice. You're asking your spouse to do something that doesn't come naturally, which requires learning a new skill. Don't take it personally if your spouse needs a reminder. Use the soft start-up each time, by defining, expressing, asserting and repeating your complaint without blame.

And remember to express gratitude when your spouse gets it right!

You can do this!

MARRIAGE RECALL

Mark what impact this topic is currently having on your marriage:

1	2	3	4	5

none *needs reminder* *needs repair*

Describe a similar experience you had relating with your spouse:

_____

_____

_____

What can you do differently using the skill outlined in this chapter?

_____

_____

_____

This week, apply your new skill and record your experience:

_____

_____

_____

_____

_____

_____

_____

Make a new mark to track your progress. Don't give up!

1	2	3	4	5

none *needs reminder* *needs repair*

REMEMBER • REPAIR • RELOVE

WEEK 3 - BATTLESHIP

Remember when you had the itch in the middle of your back; that one area that you can't reach with either hand to scratch? You asked your spouse to scratch it, and inevitably their first attempt missed. Did you tell your spouse that they hit the spot by saying something like, "Oh sweet, you got it! Thanks!" No, of course not—you gave directions. Move up a little, now left, scratch a bit harder, and move down a smidge.

This is like the game *Battleship*. You keep trying until you hit the mark.

Why didn't you pretend? Because you had a legitimate need, a willing partner, and you anticipated the moment of success.

A legitimate need. Recognize that you have legitimate needs. If you're too busy attending to everyone else's needs, take the time to identify your own needs, then ask for them to be met. Are you working very hard to deny that you have any needs at all?

Admit it, some needs *are* legitimate, and every person has them, even *you*!

A willing partner. Are you assuming your spouse isn't willing to fulfill your need, so you don't bother to ask? You could be completely wrong! The Bible states in Matthew 7:7 to, "Ask and it will be given to you." How would you act if you believed your spouse was willing? You'd hopefully invite rather than demand, give information only you could provide—with incremental instructions until...

The moment of success! Ahhhhh, oh YEAH, you got it! That moment when your spouse meets your physical, emotional, spiritual, or relational need bringing comfort, connection, resolution, satisfaction, joy, and relief! It's so good that you won't hesitate to ask again.

Many of my clients have me so delighted because they are learning to ask skillfully and respond artfully—and enjoying deep connection because of it!

Why not incorporate a game of *Battleship* into your next alone time or discussion, using simple nudges to help your spouse understand what you need, and visa-versa. It could be a fun way to communicate with each other until the target is hit.

You can do this!

MARRIAGE RECALL

Mark what impact this topic is currently having on your marriage:

1	2	3	4	5

none   *needs reminder*   *needs repair*

Describe a similar experience you had relating with your spouse:

_____

_____

_____

What can you do differently using the skill outlined in this chapter?

_____

_____

_____

This week, apply your new skill and record your experience:

_____

_____

_____

_____

_____

_____

_____

_____

Make a new mark to track your progress. Don't give up!

1	2	3	4	5

none   *needs reminder*   *needs repair*

REMEMBER • REPAIR • RELOVE

WEEK 4 - WHAT DO YOU EXPECT?

We tend to see what we expect to see. More than that, we actually help to promote what we expect to see.

For example, if I think my wife is in a bad mood because of a difficult day at work and I hear her car pull up in the driveway I might tell myself, "Now would be a good time to take the dog for a walk!" So I quickly grab the leash and hustle my dog out the back door. My wife comes in the house, she's had an average day—not great or terrible, but she wants to tell me something. She can't find me, the house is unlocked and there's no note. By the time I get back from my walk, she's irritated and has a scowl on her face. What do I tell myself? "Aha! I knew she was in a bad mood."

You see the problem; she wasn't in a bad mood. I helped to promote what I expected to see. Now let's be clear. I'm not saying that you and I are responsible for other people's behaviors. But we do have *influence*.

How are you influencing your spouse? The problem is that you may be promoting what you expect to see, rather than what you want to see. If you expect a positive outcome, you interact differently, more positively. It doesn't guarantee success, but greatly increases its likelihood. Michele Weiner-Davis, author of *Divorce Busting*, calls this technique "Act As If."

When a marriage struggles and your guard is up, what are you promoting? You can promote affection, kindness, playfulness—the good things you and your spouse signed up for when you said, "I do." You can change how you engage with your spouse by expecting warmth and cheerfulness, instead of promoting negativity by expecting the worst.

During a session with a delightful couple, the wife accused her husband of being more excited to see the dog when he came home from work than he was to see her. He said, "That's because the dog runs to the door and wags her tail when I come in." The session took a humorous twist as she practiced "wagging her tail" so that she could get it right for him in the coming days. We laughed in the session, but more importantly she started wagging her tail when he came home. It was one of the simple but significant changes that propelled them into a deeply satisfying marriage.

How would you act differently if you expected a better response? Are you willing to try? I hope so—and I hope you'll recognize significant change!

You can do this!

MARRIAGE RECALL

Mark what impact this topic is currently having on your marriage:

1	2	3	4	5

none   *needs reminder*   *needs repair*

Describe a similar experience you had relating with your spouse:

_____

_____

_____

What can you do differently using the skill outlined in this chapter?

_____

_____

_____

This week, apply your new skill and record your experience:

_____

_____

_____

_____

_____

_____

_____

Make a new mark to track your progress. Don't give up!

1	2	3	4	5

none   *needs reminder*   *needs repair*

REMEMBER • REPAIR • RELOVE

WEEK 5 - UNLOAD

Imagine you're on a long hike, and just as the trail becomes steep, even treacherous, someone hands you a 50-lb bag of rocks. What would you do? Most of us would rightfully find no value in this extra load—the journey becomes more difficult and the hike may end altogether.

Leave the bag of rocks behind.

This is so obvious, except when the bag has a resentment label plastered on it. Why would you choose to carry this extra load?

Resentment is quoted as "drinking poison and expecting someone else to get sick." This is so true. People who harbor resentment and refuse to forgive look like they've been weaned on a pickle. The poison impacts their digestive system, sleep patterns, autonomic nervous system, and muscle tension—to name a few.

Sometimes you might actually open the bag and add more rocks! When anger strikes, or disappointments grow, it seems helpful to keep that rock around for a while to show off to others—especially if the person you identify the rock with in the first place is your *spouse*.

If you harbor resentment you pay a dear price for carrying this additional load of stress, a load that *never* adds value. You don't really want to carry this extra load do you? The good news is—you don't have to!

Resentment can be let out of the bag with a healthy dose of *forgiveness*!

One of the most compelling reasons to forgive is because your spiritual vitality depends on it. Jesus linked forgiveness directly to the health of our relationship with God (Matthew 6:14-15).

Make no mistake about it, marriage reconciliation is a tough journey and you cannot afford to cut off your spiritual vitality just when the trail becomes steep.

Unload those rocks of resentment and get ready for a *lighter* walk.

You can do this!

MARRIAGE RECALL

Mark what impact this topic is currently having on your marriage:

1	2	3	4	5

none   *needs reminder*   *needs repair*

Describe a similar experience you had relating with your spouse:

_____

_____

_____

What can you do differently using the skill outlined in this chapter?

_____

_____

_____

This week, apply your new skill and record your experience:

_____

_____

_____

_____

_____

_____

_____

_____

Make a new mark to track your progress. Don't give up!

1	2	3	4	5

none   *needs reminder*   *needs repair*

REMEMBER • REPAIR • RELOVE

WEEK 6 - DEFINING FORGIVENESS

Forgiveness is a good thing, but most of us have difficulty putting it into practice. What exactly is forgiveness? How do you know when you've given or received it? These questions are important because your spiritual vitality depends on it.

It might be helpful to define what forgiveness is *not*. Forgiveness is not a feeling, though feelings are involved. Forgiveness is not saying, "What you did to me was okay." If what was done is acceptable then you're not talking about forgiveness. It's as if someone said, "If I give you $5, would you forgive me?" That doesn't make sense. The only platform for forgiveness is when something the offender has done, or has failed to do, has been harmful to you. It doesn't even matter if it was intended to be harmful. If someone runs over your foot, it hurts whether it was done intentionally or not.

Forgiveness is the decision to give up your right to make someone pay. Think about it in legal terms. If I take your car and wrap it around a tree, I owe you. You have the choice to forgive my debt by saying I don't have to pay you for the damages. However, once you surrender your right, you cannot come back later and try to make me pay. Forgiveness is your decision. You don't need anyone's help, permission, or cooperation to forgive.

It doesn't mean you're giving me the keys to your next car. This takes trust. Trust is always built through the cooperation of the person who did you harm. They make the effort to prove they are not only forgiven, but also trustworthy.

To be truly and deeply forgiving in your marriage, you need to be honest with yourself and answer the question, "How do I make my spouse pay?" If you're going to free yourself from resentment the answer to this question is key. When our boys still lived at home, I was usually the first to leave in the morning. When it snowed I left early enough to clear off everyone's car windows. However, when I held resentment I'd be sure to leave only enough time to clear off my own windows. It was subtle. No one in the family ever said, "Hey, how come you didn't clean off my car?" But I knew I was punishing them, and my resentment grew.

You may be deeply hurt. Your spouse may have treated you very badly and your resentment feels justified. But this bitterness prevents you from being the kind, loving, generous, warm person you were created to be. Don't let anything rob you of the joy and freedom that forgiveness brings. Not when it's in your power to choose freedom.

How do you make your spouse pay? When you're ready to forgive, surrender your right to exact revenge. See how much lighter and richer your life can become. It's not easy, but you're worth it!

You can do this!

MARRIAGE RECALL

Mark what impact this topic is currently having on your marriage:

1	2	3	4	5

none   *needs reminder*   *needs repair*

Describe a similar experience you had relating with your spouse:

_____

_____

_____

What can you do differently using the skill outlined in this chapter?

_____

_____

_____

This week, apply your new skill and record your experience:

_____

_____

_____

_____

_____

_____

_____

_____

Make a new mark to track your progress. Don't give up!

1	2	3	4	5

none   *needs reminder*   *needs repair*

REMEMBER • REPAIR • RELOVE

WEEK 7 - DIG A LITTLE DEEPER

The metal detector floated silently back and forth, the treasure seeker seemingly discouraged at the apparent lack of treasure on this stretch of ground. Head down, the seeker released a sigh, "I guess my friends were right, there is no hope here." All of a sudden the detector went bonkers, the needle waving wildly as the beeper screamed, "It's here! It's here under the surface! Dig here, let me show you!"

This is one of my favorite parts of being a marriage counselor and coach.

The treasure seekers are couples trying to recover the secrets to restore their marriages. The secrets are hidden beneath the surface, invisible to the untrained eye. They are within reach, but it will take a little bit of digging. So often I have the joy of uncovering evidence that these couples are on the right path, they're actually doing better than they know!

I often start a session by asking couples to tell me about progress made in their relationship since we last met. Sometimes they report no tangible progress. Then during the session they'll share positive changes and interactions. He took her to a surprise lunch. She apologized for something that hurt him. He cleaned the bathroom without being asked. She came home early from a party.

"Are these normal behaviors?" I ask. "Well, no, actually that almost never happens!" comes the response. The detector starts beeping as the needle dances wildly!

How did that happen? People change course and do things out of the ordinary for all kinds of reasons. What motivates a person to make such a decision? Human behavior is complex, and rarely does an action spring from a single stimulus. However, when your spouse does something clearly positive it is wise to reflect on how you may have influenced the switch in behavior. Perhaps you resisted the temptation to point out a mistake, or expressed appreciation for a dinner made one evening. Maybe you've just been smiling more.

Whatever you suspect had a positive impact becomes your working hypothesis. Do more of what's been working!

Are you detecting signs of progress in your relationship? Don't let them go unnoticed. Dig a little deeper. Watch the needle. It may be that you are doing better than you know!

You can do this!

MARRIAGE RECALL

Mark what impact this topic is currently having on your marriage:

1	*2*	*3*	*4*	*5*

none   *needs reminder*   *needs repair*

Describe a similar experience you had relating with your spouse:

_____

_____

_____

What can you do differently using the skill outlined in this chapter?

_____

_____

_____

This week, apply your new skill and record your experience:

_____

_____

_____

_____

_____

_____

_____

_____

Make a new mark to track your progress. Don't give up!

1	*2*	*3*	*4*	*5*

none   *needs reminder*   *needs repair*

REMEMBER • REPAIR • RELOVE

WEEK 8 - DON'T DRIBBLE THE FOOTBALL

"It's like an alien has taken over my spouse's body. It looks like my spouse, but I'm seeing actions and hearing statements that are out of left field!" I often hear this comment from a person whose spouse is going through a significant change, such as a mid-life crisis.

Facing extreme change is a chaotic time, fueled mostly by fear. It's also a complicated topic, with many facets. Let's tackle a few things that will help you love your spouse during a mid-life crisis, or other life-changing events.

It's important to realize that your spouse is primarily in an emotional state, not a rational state. It's tempting (and often way too easy) to point out the foolishness of your spouse's arguments and behaviors. Don't do it! It's not effective. Your spouse will likely see you as argumentative and unloving, then dig in their heels to hold on to their position.

Taking a rational argument into an emotional arena is like taking a football on to the basketball court. It's the wrong game with a different set of rules!

Have you ever tried to dribble a football? It's frustrating and futile! Don't waste your time and energy. I'm not suggesting you just sit back and let the new behaviors and decisions go unchallenged—not at all. Here are a couple of helpful directions to consider instead.

First, affirm how your spouse feels. This is not the same as being in agreement. For example if you hear, "I feel trapped," it's tempting to try to talk your spouse out of "feeling trapped." Instead, consider an empathetic approach that confirms how they feel by stating something like, "I've been interrogating you non-stop. No wonder you feel trapped. I'm going to make a real effort to back off."

If your spouse feels understood, the interaction will be remembered as rewarding, and that's progress. Even if you don't agree with what your spouse is doing, you must affirm how your spouse *feels*.

Second, keep in mind your spouse is still in there, somewhere! When your good-hearted, kind, intelligent, caring "real spouse" is present, feel free to engage. However, when the "alien spouse" presents itself again, don't get entangled in fruitless discussions.

Keep it friendly; just don't try to dribble the football!

You can do this!

MARRIAGE RECALL

Mark what impact this topic is currently having on your marriage:

| 1 | 2 | 3 | 4 | 5 |

none　　　　　　　　**needs reminder**　　　　　　　**needs repair**

Describe a similar experience you had relating with your spouse:

_____

_____

_____

What can you do differently using the skill outlined in this chapter?

_____

_____

_____

This week, apply your new skill and record your experience:

_____

_____

_____

_____

_____

_____

_____

_____

Make a new mark to track your progress. Don't give up!

| 1 | 2 | 3 | 4 | 5 |

none　　　　　　　　**needs reminder**　　　　　　　**needs repair**

REMEMBER · REPAIR · RELOVE

WEEK 9 - RESPECTING THE WALL

"Mr. Gorbachev, tear down this wall!" Twenty-five years ago President Ronald Reagan made this statement as part of a speech while in the shadows of the Berlin Wall. This wall separated communist-controlled East Berlin from democratic West Berlin. His words were not a threat, but an invitation. "If you seek peace, if you seek prosperity," was the prelude to his invitation. In other words, we're not going to tear down your wall, we will respect your wall. However, if you tear it down you'll enjoy something that you'll never regret.

I am often asked, "My spouse has built up a wall, how do I tear it down?" My answer is always the same. You don't! If you take a pickaxe to the wall your spouse will build it thicker and higher. My suggestion? Throw a picnic just outside of the wall!

Walls are always about safety. If you start ripping down the wall your spouse will feel less safe. You may tell me that you're the biggest teddy bear in the world, but if your spouse doesn't feel safe, you aren't going to make much progress.

So what's the picnic? It's something fun, peaceful, enjoyable, and friendly, without a high level of commitment. When your spouse joins the picnic, keep it light. Part of your spouse really longs to sit and enjoy the time. However, when your spouse's fear gets triggered (and it will), it's a race back behind the wall. Everything within you will scream, "Stop! Don't run away!" And you'll be tempted to hold on. Don't do it. If you do, your spouse will be convinced that they weren't safe at all. Then, your spouse will double their effort to stay behind the wall.

The next time your spouse is enjoying the picnic, then suddenly gets that panicked look and runs behind the wall—let go. When the door slams shut with the expectation you'll try to ram it down—stay put. Your spouse will peek through the peephole and see you at the picnic, playing some music and throwing the Frisbee to the dog. Next time, your spouse will come out sooner, and stay out longer.

When you see your spouse's wall, I encourage you to have the same message as President Reagan. "I will respect your wall, however if you come out, you'll be glad you did."

You can do this!

MARRIAGE RECALL

Mark what impact this topic is currently having on your marriage:

1	2	3	4	5

none   *needs reminder*   *needs repair*

Describe a similar experience you had relating with your spouse:

_____

_____

_____

What can you do differently using the skill outlined in this chapter?

_____

_____

_____

This week, apply your new skill and record your experience:

_____

_____

_____

_____

_____

_____

_____

_____

Make a new mark to track your progress. Don't give up!

1	2	3	4	5

none   *needs reminder*   *needs repair*

REMEMBER • REPAIR • RELOVE

WEEK 10 - WHERE'S YOUR HEART?

"The demands my spouse puts on my time are unreasonable! She knows I have this big conference coming up!" "He knew this promotion meant long hours. How can I make him understand?"

If you feel that it's not fair for your spouse to ask for more of you, you're right! It's not fair when your spouse expects you to be two places at once, to risk your job security, or to leap tall buildings in a single bound.

Busy schedules can create separation anxiety if they last too long. Don't panic. Take a deep breath and accept that life's not fair.

Now let's consider a new perspective.

When it seems like there's not enough of you to go around, take heart. Your spouse might really be asking, "Are you with me?"

Think about it. Would your spouse rather have you with them, wishing you were somewhere else? Or, have you somewhere else, wishing you were with them?

The response I always hear is, "Have me somewhere else, wishing I was with them!"

I call this *Heart Location*. Your spouse wants to know that they are in your heart. To know that your thoughts, desires, hopes, and dreams are present, no matter where you are physically.

The demands of life have you halfway there. You *are* somewhere else most of the time! The mission from here is to communicate that your heart is with your spouse.

Make this fun—use your creativity. Send a quick text message between appointments, place a sticky note on the rearview mirror, draw a heart shaped message in the snow, sneak a mint onto the pillow, tie a ribbon on their keychain, or a bow on their laptop case.

Thousands of ideas (none of which take very long) can express what your spouse needs to know: "My heart is with you."

Plan out in advance some fun ways to let your spouse know you are near, no matter how far away you are physically. What once seemed demanding can become very rewarding.

You can do this!

MARRIAGE RECALL

Mark what impact this topic is currently having on your marriage:

1	2	3	4	5

none   *needs reminder*   *needs repair*

Describe a similar experience you had relating with your spouse:

_____

_____

_____

What can you do differently using the skill outlined in this chapter?

_____

_____

_____

This week, apply your new skill and record your experience:

_____

_____

_____

_____

_____

_____

_____

Make a new mark to track your progress. Don't give up!

1	2	3	4	5

none   *needs reminder*   *needs repair*

REMEMBER · REPAIR · RELOVE

WEEK 11 - TRANSFORMATION

Two of my favorite movies are *It's A Wonderful Life* and *The Wizard of Oz*. It's interesting that at the end of these stories the main characters end up in exactly the same place as they were at the beginning.

Dorothy wakes up back in the dusty routine of farm life. George returns to his hinge-pin role at the old Building and Loan.

Nothing's changed, but everything's different. This is transformation!

The most poignant picture of this is when George Bailey interacts with the loose staircase knob. When the knob came off in George's hand, before meeting his guardian angel, he's ready to throw it through a window! Do you remember how he responded to the loose knob after his transformation? That's right, he kissed it and joyfully returned it to its proper place.

The knob stayed the same, but George had an internal change.

As he proceeded up the stairs, his kids—who earlier withdrew from him in fear—climbed on him like a litter of kittens.

My favorite clients, the ones who inspire me to be a better man, husband, dad, and counselor, have this characteristic in common—they don't demand circumstances submit to their wills. They take life on life's terms. They seek the kind of transformation that enables them to experience the very same circumstances from a fresh, hope-filled, life-affirming perspective.

The irony is that their transformed attitude often influences their circumstances.

One of the best ways to identify if you are in transformation is from the questions you ask. "How can I get my spouse to…" is a pre-transformational question. It focuses on the other person. "How can I respond more lovingly when…" is a good indicator that you're growing through your trials and embracing transformation.

I am convinced that the spouse who knows that nothing has changed, but can see that everything can be different becomes a greater influence —a hope-filled, life-affirming influence— toward a successful and thriving marriage.

You can do this!

MARRIAGE RECALL

Mark what impact this topic is currently having on your marriage:

1	*2*	*3*	*4*	*5*

none   *needs reminder*   *needs repair*

Describe a similar experience you had relating with your spouse:

_____

_____

_____

What can you do differently using the skill outlined in this chapter?

_____

_____

_____

This week, apply your new skill and record your experience:

_____

_____

_____

_____

_____

_____

Make a new mark to track your progress. Don't give up!

1	*2*	*3*	*4*	*5*

none   *needs reminder*   *needs repair*

REMEMBER • REPAIR • RELOVE

WEEK 12 - TURN AROUND

Are you willing to try things that don't make sense, that make you uncomfortable, that feel like the wrong direction?

I live just east of the foothills leading to the Rocky Mountains. Directions here are easy—the mountains are always west. Recently I traveled to California for a conference where the mountains were always east. For three days my internal compass was backwards. I drove north to the conference, placing the mountains on my right. Everything within me wanted to keep them on my left, which of course would be the absolute wrong direction!

Where is *your* marital compass pointing?

I am convinced you want to reach a good destination. Couples usually want clearer communication, passionate affection, sound financial management, laughter—and more fun. However, when your compass is pointing in the wrong direction, your destination gets further and further away. This is when you can be tempted to give up!

Please don't give up until you at least consider the possibility that your map is upside down! Right becomes wrong, and up actually points down.

Believe me, driving north with the mountains on my right just felt wrong, but I couldn't argue with the results. I arrived at my destination, and on time!

It's time to turn your map around and get headed in the right direction.

Michele Weiner-Davis, author of *Divorce Busting*, calls this "doing a 180." Doing a 180 might feel wrong, but to reach your destination you need to turn around and go the opposite direction.

Jesus often flipped things around in ways that didn't seem to make sense. "If you want to be first, go to the back of the line." "If you want to be the master, start washing people's feet." "If you want to gain your life, lose it."

Could it be that living a healthy, spiritually mature life requires facing another direction and going the opposite way, even if it feels uncomfortable?

Find new ways to reach the goals you have for your marriage. Consider couples counseling or go on a retreat, read *Divorce Busting*, or other books on marriage, sign up for dancing lessons, or write a love letter. Do *something* different.

How's your marital compass? Are your efforts moving you further from your destination? If so, turning your map around might help get you where you want to be—and on time!

You can do this!

MARRIAGE RECALL

Mark what impact this topic is currently having on your marriage:

1	*2*	*3*	*4*	*5*
none		*needs reminder*		*needs repair*

Describe a similar experience you had relating with your spouse:

_____

_____

_____

What can you do differently using the skill outlined in this chapter?

_____

_____

_____

This week, apply your new skill and record your experience:

_____

_____

_____

_____

_____

_____

_____

Make a new mark to track your progress. Don't give up!

1	*2*	*3*	*4*	*5*
none		*needs reminder*		*needs repair*

REMEMBER • REPAIR • RELOVE

WEEK 13 - MR. NICE GUY

"Hello, my name is Chuck, and I am a recovering nice guy." When I was a kid, my mom told me, "If you don't have anything nice to say, don't say anything at all." I didn't talk for a week! I grew up believing that negative feelings were not to be expressed. If I ignored them, maybe they would just go away. However, when I stuffed my feelings, they seemed to burst out of me at the worst possible time. Then I discovered the trick that would release my pent up negative emotions: *Sarcastic humor to the rescue!*

If I make a sarcastic comment, and you take offense—apparently you're just too sensitive! I can express my irritation with my spouse, hide behind the "just kidding" shield, and never have to reveal who I am or what I really want.

When I met my quick-witted wife, Jan, we laughed often and fully. But her humor wasn't harmful or attacking. This exposed my hurtful, defensive style of humor. I felt vulnerable, not knowing quite what to do with my negative emotions. I returned to "not saying anything at all."

I decided to be Mr. Nice Guy. I would just go along for the ride, internally pledging to never rock the boat, and say, "yes" to everything. Who wouldn't love this guy?

I thought "nice" was loving. Instead being silent often communicated negative, unintended messages. "I won't let you know me." "I don't trust you." "You're not important enough for me to engage with."

Communication experts say that people cannot *not* communicate. Even silence bears a message. If you let silence speak for you it will often say things you don't intend—and you become accountable for things you never even thought.

If you're facing a silent partner, you can't really know what your spouse is thinking. In fact, you have the freedom to interpret the silence however you want. Why not choose to believe something good? "My spouse is stunned by my brilliance." "My spouse agrees with my decision to buy that new couch." Your positive approach is more inviting, and will help keep the door of communication open.

Expressing negative thoughts takes courage. I'm still learning how to stumble through my words, and face the outcome—embracing the fact that it's better to be "real" than to be "nice." If you're leaning on being "nice" through silence, take the courageous step of saying something "real" instead, even if it's, "I don't know how I feel about that right now."

Break the silence by revealing who you are and what you really want. It matters to you and your spouse.

You can do this!

MARRIAGE RECALL

Mark what impact this topic is currently having on your marriage:

1	2	3	4	5

none   *needs reminder*   *needs repair*

Describe a similar experience you had relating with your spouse:

_____

_____

_____

What can you do differently using the skill outlined in this chapter?

_____

_____

_____

This week, apply your new skill and record your experience:

_____

_____

_____

_____

_____

_____

_____

Make a new mark to track your progress. Don't give up!

1	2	3	4	5

none   *needs reminder*   *needs repair*

REMEMBER • REPAIR • RELOVE

WEEK 14 - DO NOT RUN!

Fear is a powerful motivator, but it's a pretty lousy guide. Living in Colorado I've had the privilege of hiking in the Rocky Mountains. You don't get very far on a trail before you come across a sign that states, "You Are Now In Bear Country!" This is followed by a list of rules for survival. One rule on the list states, "If you see a bear DO NOT RUN." The experts know that I cannot outrun a bear. They also know that if I run, I could trigger a "chase response" in the bear and end up with the very thing I don't want—a bear breathing down my neck!

The same is true in relationships. When my primary motivation is fear, very likely I'm about to do something that points me in the wrong direction. In fact, it may be leading me to the very thing I don't want. It's a great time to ask the question, "What would happen if I didn't do what fear wants me to do right now?"

I've seen fear prompt behaviors that are harmful to relationships. Calling and leaving seventeen messages in an hour is usually fear-based. Interrogating your spouse for 40 minutes when they are 20 minutes late is usually fear-based. Checking phone records, putting a tracking device in the car, breaking into email accounts, hiding money in a secret stash—these are all usually fear-based behaviors that often backfire.

Fear-based relating is as old as, well, Adam and Eve! The Bible states in Genesis 3:10 that after they had eaten the forbidden fruit, Adam said to God, "I heard you in the garden, and I was afraid because I was naked; so I hid." Fear has been a hindrance to relationships ever since!

So what should we do about fear? First, realize that you're going to feel afraid at times, that's normal. But we can choose to respond differently to our own fear by asking, "What would I be doing if I had no fear right now?" The bear experts tell us, "Do not run! Make yourself look bigger. Back away slowly. Speak gently! Look for rocks and sticks to defend yourself if the bear charges." In other words, act differently than you feel.

The next time you are triggered to react out of fear, DO NOT RUN! Instead, have a plan to respond differently and increase your chance of success.

You can do this!

MARRIAGE RECALL

Mark what impact this topic is currently having on your marriage:

1	2	3	4	5
none		*needs reminder*		*needs repair*

Describe a similar experience you had relating with your spouse:

_____

_____

_____

What can you do differently using the skill outlined in this chapter?

_____

_____

_____

This week, apply your new skill and record your experience:

_____

_____

_____

_____

_____

_____

_____

Make a new mark to track your progress. Don't give up!

1	2	3	4	5
none		*needs reminder*		*needs repair*

REMEMBER · REPAIR · RELOVE

WEEK 15 - LAUGH

"How much laughter do you get throughout your day?" I ask this question often when I work with couples. It's a tough question to answer when your marriage is really struggling.

"I don't feel like laughing," or "Nothing funny is going on here," are common responses. However, marriage reconciliation requires us to be at our best—and laughter is a key ingredient.

The benefits of laughter are physical, mental, and social.

Physically, laughter boosts your immunity, lowers stress hormones, decreases pain, relaxes your muscles, and helps prevent heart disease.

Mentally, laughter adds joy and zest to life, eases anxiety and fear, relieves stress, improves mood, and enhances resilience.

Socially, laughter strengthens relationships, attracts others, enhances teamwork, helps defuse conflict, and promotes group bonding.

Laughter is a unique commodity. It's free, you can do it alone, and the things you can find to bring a smile to your face are limitless. Studies show even forced laughter can make you feel better, because your body still releases endorphins, which relieve stress.

My wife and I have been able to weave laughter into our interactions—even during high-stress discussions. It helps balance our response to hard topics, and reminds us we are on the same team.

I go so far as to tell clients that if your spouse calls and you don't have a smile on your face let it go to voicemail. Don't even read a text message or email unless you're smiling, because laughter not only impacts how you present to the world, but also *how you perceive* the world around you.

First, spend a few minutes watching your favorite comedian, reading the comics, playing with the dogs, or watching another online video about cats! Do something that makes you crack a smile and genuinely laugh. Then, listen to the message from your spouse with a new perspective, and see how it impacts the outcome.

Laughter has always been called the best medicine for good reason!

You can do this!

MARRIAGE RECALL

Mark what impact this topic is currently having on your marriage:

1	2	3	4	5

none   *needs reminder*   *needs repair*

Describe a similar experience you had relating with your spouse:

_____

_____

_____

What can you do differently using the skill outlined in this chapter?

_____

_____

_____

This week, apply your new skill and record your experience:

_____

_____

_____

_____

_____

_____

_____

Make a new mark to track your progress. Don't give up!

1	2	3	4	5

none   *needs reminder*   *needs repair*

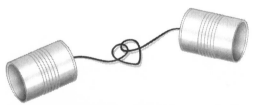

REMEMBER • REPAIR • RELOVE

WEEK 16 - ME OVERREACT? NEVER!

"I can't handle all the drama. My spouse overreacts to everything!" I hear this complaint regularly during counseling. "But what if your spouse *isn't* overreacting? What if your spouse is having a perfectly appropriate response to a stimulus you simply do not see?"

I'm not presenting this as the gospel truth, but I challenge you to consider the possibility.

For instance, let's say you spent the morning trimming bushes and trees around the yard and unknowingly picked up a splinter. You come into the house, grab a glass of water at the wrong angle and it pushes the splinter into a waiting nerve ending that screams to your brain, "Get me out of here!" as your arm obediently jerks backward.

Do you stop in that moment and say, "Wow, I sure overreacted to that! After all, it's only a glass of water!" Of course not—because you were responding appropriately to the *pain*.

We can waste a lot of time judging emotions with common expressions like, "You shouldn't feel like that," or, "Don't be such a drama queen."

Do they work? If you're honest enough to admit it you know these rarely advance toward a solution. Instead, they typically trigger defensive and heels-dug-in comments like, "Don't you tell me how I should feel!"

The next time your spouse "overreacts" how could you respond if you believed the emotion was perfectly appropriate? What could you do differently to empathize with the pain behind the emotion; instead of assuming it was out of line? Would you show interest? Demonstrate compassion? Be patient and kind? Give this some thought and then practice with conviction, so you have confidence when your spouse "overreacts" the next time.

A good place to start is by asking for more information. Remember, you can't see the stimulus, so you need some help to understand. "What happened? You're really upset! Can I do anything to help?" Then listen for the "splinter" that is causing the emotion.

You don't have to overreact to your spouse's overreaction! You and your spouse may both find some profound relief that comes from removing emotional splinters—and enter into a deeper place of connection.

You can do this!

MARRIAGE RECALL

Mark what impact this topic is currently having on your marriage:

1	2	3	4	5

none   *needs reminder*   *needs repair*

Describe a similar experience you had relating with your spouse:

_____

_____

_____

What can you do differently using the skill outlined in this chapter?

_____

_____

_____

This week, apply your new skill and record your experience:

_____

_____

_____

_____

_____

_____

_____

_____

Make a new mark to track your progress. Don't give up!

1	2	3	4	5

none   *needs reminder*   *needs repair*

REMEMBER · REPAIR · RELOVE

WEEK 17 - CAPICHE?

Capiche? In 1940s slang, the word *capiche* derived from the Italian word *capisci*, meaning, "Do you understand?"

Many couples come to my office and exclaim, "We just don't communicate!" I suspect what my troubled clients really mean is that they are failing to *understand*. It is possible to hear the words and yet entirely miss the heart.

The Bible states in James 1:19 for us to be, "quick to listen, slow to speak, and slow to become angry." This is a very intentional process that is especially helpful with emotionally charged areas in marriage, such as, parenting, sex, finances, in-laws, and other hot topics.

Let's focus solely on being "quick to listen." I am convinced that skillful listening has the power to turn around marriages that are really hurting.

Most people consider themselves to be pretty good listeners. However, hearing comes naturally and is effortless, but listening takes focus and practice. Active listening is more than just hearing your spouse's words. Active listening pursues your spouse's heart; it gives your spouse the gift of empathy.

Many couples have some experience with the "speaker-listener technique" often taught in seminars, counseling sessions, or marriage retreats. The concept is simple. First, the speaker follows the Speaker Guidelines:

- Describe the stressful situation and express how you felt. Keep your statements brief, within 3 to 5 sentences.
- Use "I" statements to maintain ownership of your experience.
- Then, give the listener the opportunity to reflect back to you what they heard.

As the listener you have one goal—to relay back what was said and convince the speaker that you heard them correctly using the Listener Guidelines:

- Make eye contact as you reflect what you heard back to the speaker.
- Do not agree, disagree, debate or negotiate—just relay back what you heard.
- Focus on the emotion words, such as "embarrassed," "angry," "lonely," and "afraid." Recognize what your spouse felt in the situation.
- Feel free to ask questions to get clarification.
- Watch the speaker for nonverbal cues that indicate you heard correctly, especially head nodding and eye contact.

How do you know when you've achieved empathy and true understanding? When you can tell your spouse's story from your *spouse's* perspective! That's when you *capiche*, and your spouse feels heard, understood, honored, loved, and respected.

You can do this!

Mark what impact this topic is currently having on your marriage:

1	*2*	*3*	*4*	*5*

none   *needs reminder*   *needs repair*

Describe a similar experience you had relating with your spouse:

_____

_____

_____

What can you do differently using the skill outlined in this chapter?

_____

_____

_____

This week, apply your new skill and record your experience:

_____

_____

_____

_____

_____

_____

_____

Make a new mark to track your progress. Don't give up!

1	*2*	*3*	*4*	*5*

none   *needs reminder*   *needs repair*

REMEMBER • REPAIR • RELOVE

WEEK 18 - DEAFENING SILENCE

~~~~~~

If you've read the chapter on active listening (*Capiche!*, page 79), you might have thought, "I would love to listen—if my spouse would ever say anything!" This can be particularly painful if your spouse talks to others, like friends or family, but doesn't share much with you.

Silence often happens when a spouse is either an avoider (one who has learned to disconnect from emotions) or a pleaser (one who is tuned into everyone else's emotions but not their own).

How can you actively listen when your spouse is silent?

Prepare to listen. Make sure that your resentment levels are low. Resentment's sole purpose for existing is to make someone pay for your hurts, and it doesn't create a safe setting that feels inviting to your spouse. Resentment will find expression unless you remove it through forgiveness. Also, use wisdom. If both of you are early risers, don't initiate a deep conversation late at night when you're both tired. If you're facing a stress-filled Wednesday, don't have the discussion on Tuesday. Finally, remove as many distractions as possible. Turn off the TV and cell phone, and send the kids over to a friend's house. Give yourself a real chance at success.

Choose safe topics. If your marriage is really hurting, I suggest you treat the dialog as if you were speaking to your sibling instead of your spouse. Choose safe topics such as the weather, upcoming business meetings, the kids' newest adventure, or how disappointing your favorite sports team has been. These are all are fair game. You wouldn't typically talk to your sibling about improving your relationship, so don't start there with your spouse.

If your spouse brings a heated topic up, try to listen non-defensively. This is where the active listening technique can help. And don't interrupt! Many of us are unaware how often we derail a conversation because we talk instead of listen. This is especially critical if your spouse hesitates to talk in the first place.

Enhance the conversation with questions. There are generally two styles of questions. One style says, "I'm really interested, tell me more about you," and the other says, "I'm taking notes so you better have your facts straight!"

Which style do you think has a better success rate? Better yet, which style did you use when you were first smitten by this fascinating creature? Try *that* style again. Generally speaking, if my question is inspired by curiosity, it probably has a better chance of success than if it's motivated by fear. "Hey, how was that new band last night?" is probably better than "Why were you out so late, again?"

Focus on patient, non-defensive listening and you may be surprised by the stories you will hear—both in number and in depth.

You can do this!

MARRIAGE RECALL

Mark what impact this topic is currently having on your marriage:

1	2	3	4	5
none		*needs reminder*		*needs repair*

Describe a similar experience you had relating with your spouse:

_____

_____

_____

What can you do differently using the skill outlined in this chapter?

_____

_____

_____

This week, apply your new skill and record your experience:

_____

_____

_____

_____

_____

_____

_____

_____

Make a new mark to track your progress. Don't give up!

1	2	3	4	5
none		*needs reminder*		*needs repair*

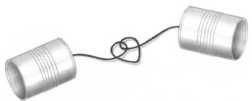

REMEMBER · REPAIR · RELOVE

WEEK 19 - DON'T BLAME ME!

"It's not my fault!"

This statement often comes from a client who has harmed their spouse. I admit, when I hear, "It's not my fault," I usually respond with suspicion. "Really? Are you sure? Then, why are you defending yourself?"

But as I listen to stories of childhood neglect, trauma, and abuse that many of my clients have endured, I'm more convinced that they may be right. The irrational beliefs, absurd fears, and harmful styles of relating from an abusive past may not be your fault—but they are your problem!

Many people have been raised on a steady diet of rejection establishing beliefs that they are not, "good enough," "smart enough," "pretty enough," or "athletic enough." Flat out *not enough*!

Others have been scarred by a consistent message of disdain. "I wish you were never born." "You'll never amount to anything."

"Why are you so stupid?" "You're too needy. My life would be so much better without you."

The real damage occurs when the statements are perpetuated as truth and you continue to tell yourself the same things.

The Bible tells us in 1 Corinthians 13:11, "When I was a child, I talked like a child, I thought like a child, I reasoned like a child. When I became a man, I put the ways of childhood behind me." As a child you didn't have the capacity to challenge hurtful lies, so you grew up with them and did what you could to survive. And you made it! Now, it's time to put away childish things.

When my client says, "It's not my fault," I hear "I'm not willing to change my behavior."

Taking responsibility for how you treat your spouse, even if you have endured hurtful words and actions as part of your past, helps you take a deep wound and change it into a *solvable problem*.

Are you willing to battle for what is right? To set yourself free from the lies that have kept you stuck in the past?

By owning your problems, even if they are not your fault, you may also stop the harm you inflict on your current relationship. You might uncover a marriage that is more rewarding than you ever imagined.

You can do this!

MARRIAGE RECALL

Mark what impact this topic is currently having on your marriage:

1	2	3	4	5

none   *needs reminder*   *needs repair*

Describe a similar experience you had relating with your spouse:

_____

_____

_____

What can you do differently using the skill outlined in this chapter?

_____

_____

_____

This week, apply your new skill and record your experience:

_____

_____

_____

_____

_____

_____

_____

_____

Make a new mark to track your progress. Don't give up!

1	2	3	4	5

none   *needs reminder*   *needs repair*

REMEMBER · REPAIR · RELOVE

WEEK 20 - MINDREADING (IS) FOR DUMMIES

I can't even count how many times I've heard clients say "I'm not a mind-reader, but..." This is usually followed by the assumption that my client knows exactly what their spouse is thinking. Unfortunately, the assumption is often wrong!

I've observed a few things about mind-reading.

First, the interpretation the mind-reader gives is almost always negative. "She thinks I'm stupid," or "He's pretending to be nice because he wants to impress my family."

Second, the spouse whose mind has been "read" often becomes defensive. "Don't put words in my mouth! That's NOT what I meant!" If this goes on long enough, your spouse might stop trying to communicate altogether!

Mind-reading is for dummies! It's also a huge roadblock to healing a hurting marriage. The key to overcome the impulse to mind-read is to replace it with *ownership*.

If you are a mind-reader, ask yourself if your thoughts are speculative. Did your spouse *actually say* what you think? If your wife said you were stupid 10 years ago, and it stung—you might be carrying a past hurt into the present. Understand that you could have a tainted recollection.

This leads to the underlying issue! Your spouse has also said that you're smart, brave, kind, and generous at different times in your marriage. Why aren't these the thoughts that come to your mind?

Mind-reading is often negative because it's motivated by fear. I'm afraid "my wife thinks I'm stupid." I'm afraid "my husband's pretending to be nice because he want to impress my family."

If you're on the receiving end of mind-reading, understand that your spouse is *afraid*. Fear is what motivates the erroneous interpretation of your behavior. You can argue, but it'll likely increase fear and solidify your spouse's interpretation.

You also need to take ownership. Your spouse did not create this belief in a vacuum. You've contributed.

Consider how you helped your spouse get here. Offer words of ownership such as, "I understand why you don't feel important to me, especially when I didn't defend you from my family's harsh words," or "I'd have a hard time feeling secure too—after all the criticism I've thrown at you."

Your response can promote safety, which invites your spouse to engage with trust instead of fear. Don't be a dummy! It's often the small changes in interactions that lead the relationship down a new path.

You can do this!

MARRIAGE RECALL

Mark what impact this topic is currently having on your marriage:

1	2	3	4	5

none   *needs reminder*   *needs repair*

Describe a similar experience you had relating with your spouse:

_____

_____

_____

What can you do differently using the skill outlined in this chapter?

_____

_____

_____

This week, apply your new skill and record your experience:

_____

_____

_____

_____

_____

_____

_____

Make a new mark to track your progress. Don't give up!

1	2	3	4	5

none   *needs reminder*   *needs repair*

REMEMBER · REPAIR · RELOVE

WEEK 21 - HOW TO BE NAKED IN MARRIAGE

Step One—take off all of your clothes

Step Two—uh, I guess you're done. WRONG!

In marriage, physical nakedness is easy to accomplish (see Step One), but for a deeply satisfying marriage you need to move toward emotional, intellectual, spiritual, as well as physical nakedness.

In marriage, nakedness isn't about being seen, it's about being *known*.

Being known by your spouse requires that you address two areas of relating: the hidden area (things that you know about yourself that others don't know) and the blind area (things that others know about you that you don't know about yourself).

Shrinking the hidden area requires courage. The hidden area is where you store things you know about yourself that your spouse doesn't know. Some of these are painful, traumatic experiences that you've endured; others are shameful things that you have said and done; still others are hopes and dreams that you embrace but are embarrassed to share. When a hidden area is threatened to be exposed, you can feel anything from low-level anxiety to full-blown panic. It's tempting to pick up a mask to hide behind, especially if you've used anger, humor, or withdrawal to hide. But these responses bring very little hope for connection, love, and intimacy. Somewhere deep within, you really long to be known, but it can be scary. Take a risk, share something hidden with your spouse.

Shrinking the blind area requires feedback. Your spouse knows things about you that you yourself don't even know! Think about it, hundreds of people know what the back of your head looks like, but you've never directly seen it! Your spouse has important information about you that can help you to grow, but it's not always pleasant to hear. Be approachable and request your spouse's input. Maybe you should start with the tough questions that you typically avoid. "What have I done this week that has been irritating?" "When do you feel safe with me?" "When do you feel unsafe?" "If you could magically change one thing about me, what would it be?"

When you're ready to tackle one of these, be wise. If you're an early bird, don't start this conversation at midnight. If your spouse has a stressful meeting Wednesday morning, don't have this conversation Tuesday night. Give yourself a real opportunity for success in being known, and then have fun getting naked!

You can do this!

MARRIAGE RECALL

Mark what impact this topic is currently having on your marriage:

1	2	3	4	5

none   *needs reminder*   *needs repair*

Describe a similar experience you had relating with your spouse:

_____

_____

_____

What can you do differently using the skill outlined in this chapter?

_____

_____

_____

This week, apply your new skill and record your experience:

_____

_____

_____

_____

_____

_____

_____

Make a new mark to track your progress. Don't give up!

1	2	3	4	5

none   *needs reminder*   *needs repair*

REMEMBER • REPAIR • RELOVE

WEEK 22 - DISAGREE (WITHOUT BEING DISAGREEABLE)

Conflict is an area that often motivates a couple to seek counseling. Parenting issues, division of duties, financial goals, and everyday life can all be sources of disagreement.

Differing conflict resolution styles can add to the challenge. Often, one spouse is a *fighter*—a person who likes to tackle conflict head on, get it resolved, and get back to enjoyable interaction. The faster the better, let's get 'er *done!*

Nothing is wrong with this style of resolving conflict. The problem comes when a *fighter* marries... a *runner!*

The *runner* feels the hair stand up on the back of their neck whenever conflict arises. A *runner* needs some space to take time to gather their thoughts so they can speak without regrets. Nothing is wrong with this conflict style either.

The tug of war begins *between* the two styles. Something has to give!

During a class I taught on marriage conflict a student shared, "My wife and I struggle during conflict. We'll be talking about something important, not even heated, and she'll just up and walk out of the room! I can't believe how disrespectful she is!" Then I asked a question I already knew the answer to, "What do you do when she leaves the room?" He said, "Well, I follow her." "Does that help?" I asked. "No, it usually makes it worse. What should I do?"

My highly trained mind came up with an immediate answer. "Do something different! Watch TV, go for a walk, tinker in the garage—do *anything* but follow her. Do you think you can do that?" He had to think for a second. Then agreed, "Yes, I think I can."

The next week he came to class with a big smile on his face. "I had a chance to practice what we talked about," he said. Translation: He and his wife got into an argument. She stormed out of the room and he took a few steps to follow her. Then he stopped, took a deep breath, and sat down to read the newspaper instead. Five minutes later his wife came back and said, "I was so mad I stomped up to our room and slammed the door in your face, but... your face wasn't there! I was so worried, I had to come back and see if you were okay." When she saw him calmly reading the paper, she decided it was safe, and they came to a resolution! (*Disclaimer—Results may vary!*)

Are you and your spouse fighting the same fights over and over, ending up in the same place? Take it from a highly trained professional, as a *fighter* or a *runner*—you'll need to be creative, and have a plan in mind before the next heated conversation. Eliminate the option that you already know doesn't work, and take another path.

You can do this!

MARRIAGE RECALL

Mark what impact this topic is currently having on your marriage:

1	2	3	4	5

none   *needs reminder*   *needs repair*

Describe a similar experience you had relating with your spouse:

_____

_____

_____

What can you do differently using the skill outlined in this chapter?

_____

_____

_____

This week, apply your new skill and record your experience:

_____

_____

_____

_____

_____

_____

_____

Make a new mark to track your progress. Don't give up!

1	2	3	4	5

none   *needs reminder*   *needs repair*

REMEMBER * REPAIR * RELOVE

WEEK 23 - OH NO! I'M HUNGRY!

In the movie *Serenity*, an experiment is done to remove all hostility and aggression in humans. The results of the experiment were that people stopped. Sure, they stopped fighting, but they also stopped caring. They stopped going to work. They stopped loving, eating, moving—they stopped *living*.

I believe that dissatisfaction plays a key role in our lives. It moves us to action.

The pattern may be easiest to see in your physical life. You get hungry, that is, you are dissatisfied with the current condition of your digestive system. This moves you to eat something, to recharge yourself physically. *Ahhh!* You return to a state of satisfaction, contentment, and relief. You don't question if something's wrong with you when you're hungry. You accept this as a normal, healthy part of living. The dissatisfaction moves you to do something good.

However, when a hint of dissatisfaction in your relationship grows, it can send you and your spouse into a huge tailspin.

"Here we go again!" I hear my clients say. They feel so defeated, back to square one, with all progress lost. This is often when fear-based decisions are made that lead to desperation and then more fear. It can spiral downward in a hurry.

What if discontent simply means you're hungry for more *good* in your marriage? How would you approach your situation differently?

The first battle to be won is in your mind. Zig Ziglar said, "We need a check-up from the neck up to avoid stinkin' thinkin'." Capturing your thoughts is important because you respond to what you put in your mind—whether it's true or not.

Close your eyes and imagine your favorite meal. You see the steam rising. You can almost smell the aroma. Even though no plate of delicious food is present, you will actually begin to salivate! You prepare to act according to your *thoughts*.

When negative thoughts are entertained, responses line up with them. "She thinks I'm stupid!" and "He doesn't love me," can turn your face to a scowl, lead you to argue or withdraw, or turn to an addiction for comfort. Stinkin' thinkin' points in the wrong direction.

What if your marital dissatisfaction led to thoughts like this instead? "I'm hungry for more affection!" "It would be great to have another serving of playfulness." "I should have recreation every week!" "Please pass me more reassurance." How would you respond differently? You might replace scowls with smiles, have more open eye contact, and reach out with gentle touches and affirming words. That sounds like a banquet to enjoy!

You can do this!

MARRIAGE RECALL

Mark what impact this topic is currently having on your marriage:

1	2	3	4	5

none   *needs reminder*   *needs repair*

Describe a similar experience you had relating with your spouse:

_____

_____

_____

What can you do differently using the skill outlined in this chapter?

_____

_____

_____

This week, apply your new skill and record your experience:

_____

_____

_____

_____

_____

_____

_____

Make a new mark to track your progress. Don't give up!

1	2	3	4	5

none   *needs reminder*   *needs repair*

REMEMBER · REPAIR · RELOVE

WEEK 24 - THIS IS MY EXIT

Anger can be like a truck barreling uncontrollably down a mountainside. Damage is going to be done to your relationship unless you immediately find a runaway-truck ramp!

Preventative measures can help keep anger from escalating. For instance, taking time for more exercise to relieve stress, or, saving difficult discussions for when you're well rested, giving them the best chance for success. However, once you realize the truck is picking up speed and the brakes aren't holding—you need an *exit strategy*.

First, identify that you're getting heated. This seems like it should be easy enough to recognize, but if your spouse is the one pointing it out with statements like, "Why don't you just calm down!"—you might not accept that you're headed for trouble.

People feel emotionally overwhelmed when they enter a measurable emotional state called "flooding." Physiologically, your body is responding to stress by releasing adrenaline into your system, draining blood from your brain to send to your major muscle groups. You are in a "fight or flight" mode without the capacity to make sound decisions! This is the place where people say and do things they regret.

How do you know when you're flooded? One practical way is to take your resting heart rate, then add 20%. At 60 beats per minute, 20% would be 72 beats per minute. If your pulse reaches 72 bpm, there's a good chance you're flooded, and exiting is essential.

Plan an exit phrase with your spouse. Using a signal like, "I need to go lay down for a while. Let's talk about this in about an hour," gives you time to regroup without abandoning the discussion. Once you've exited your goal is to *regain your calm*.

Start with controlled breathing. Inhale deeply, hold for a few seconds, and then exhale slowly. Do this several times to send the message to your body, "I'm OK!"

Find the tension in your body and intentionally release it. Some people get tense shoulders or a knot in their stomach, others grind their teeth. Try to increase the tension in the area that affects you by flexing those muscles for a few seconds, and then let them go as you relax.

Capture your thoughts. What were you thinking when your heart started racing? Challenge your thoughts with the question, "Is what I think about this *true?*"

Remember, you need to get the truck back on the road. These important topics need to be discussed, just not now. Regain your calm, gather your thoughts, and get professional help if needed.

You'll have the opportunity to enter the on ramp with constructive conversation again soon.

You can do this!

MARRIAGE RECALL

Mark what impact this topic is currently having on your marriage:

1	2	3	4	5

none　　　　　　*needs reminder*　　　　　*needs repair*

Describe a similar experience you had relating with your spouse:

_____

_____

_____

What can you do differently using the skill outlined in this chapter?

_____

_____

_____

This week, apply your new skill and record your experience:

_____

_____

_____

_____

_____

_____

_____

_____

Make a new mark to track your progress. Don't give up!

1	2	3	4	5

none　　　　　　*needs reminder*　　　　　*needs repair*

SECTION TWO - REPAIR

REMEMBER • **REPAIR** • RELOVE

REMEMBER • **REPAIR** • RELOVE

WEEK 25 - FOCUS ON THE VALUE

If your spouse has told you, "I love you, but I'm not *in love* with you," it can cause you to panic and take steps that could make matters worse. Some typical reactions are to prompt an immediate action such as, "Let's go see a counselor," or "Please read this book on marriage with me," or "Let's get to work on our relationship." If you've tried these options and they've been productive, keep doing them. However, usually by the time a declaration of this sort is made they tend to push the spouse further away.

These are chasing behaviors. And if you want your spouse to stop running, *stop chasing!*

Instead, focus on the value. All of these actions cost your spouse something—time, energy, money, effort, or emotional risk. These are all positive actions, but if your spouse doesn't see the value, they're not going to pay the price.

Consider the car salesman. When you walk on to the lot he doesn't walk you up to the most expensive car and point at the sticker price.

He sits you in the car and encourages you to feel the leather, take it for a drive, experience the handling, and listen to the surround-sound. He's trying to get you to experience the value because if you do you're more likely to pay the price. Let your spouse experience the value of being in the relationship with you.

First, find out what your spouse values. Begin simply with a smile, a word of gratitude or a kind gesture. Gary Chapman's book, *The 5 Love Languages*, will help you understand your spouse's love language. Whether the language is words of affirmation, acts of service, receiving gifts, quality time, or physical touch—learn to speak it *fluently*.

If your spouse has a wall up, don't expect the first few attempts to get through. Be patient and consistent as you practice learning how to better love your spouse.

Your new focus will be tested. But don't worry! You can identify upcoming tests, and learn how to pass them.

For now, focus on the value!

You can do this!

MARRIAGE RECALL

Mark what impact this topic is currently having on your marriage:

1	*2*	*3*	*4*	*5*

none   *needs reminder*   *needs repair*

Describe a similar experience you had relating with your spouse:

_____

_____

_____

What can you do differently using the skill outlined in this chapter?

_____

_____

_____

This week, apply your new skill and record your experience:

_____

_____

_____

_____

_____

_____

_____

Make a new mark to track your progress. Don't give up!

1	*2*	*3*	*4*	*5*

none   *needs reminder*   *needs repair*

REMEMBER • **REPAIR** • RELOVE

WEEK 26 - IDENTIFY THE TEST

It's essential to understand that the good, healthy, positive changes that you're making probably won't be embraced immediately. Sometimes they'll seem to irritate your spouse. The changes will be tested.

This is more than okay. I believe it's essential for the long-term success of your reconciliation efforts. Let me explain how to identify tests, and more importantly, how to pass them!

Every disgruntled spouse has a few core beliefs that give them confidence that they can walk away from the marriage.

First, your spouse believes who you are holds no mystery. They believe they know what you like, what you don't like, and how you're going to respond to any situation. Second, your spouse believes that you will never significantly change. But, when you start your reconciliation effort in earnest, you're going to give your spouse a "new you." You're done with the same "old you" that your spouse expects.

You're going to relate differently. This challenges the core beliefs of your spouse, and creates a problem. Part of your spouse will respond with, "Oh, this is so nice! I have longed for this type of interaction!" But another part—the protective part—responds, "Are you crazy? Don't you remember this is the person who said X, did Y, and forgot to do Z?" This leads your spouse to review their list of complaints, and let's face it, you've given your spouse some real reasons to complain! This internal struggle is a good problem because it means that your spouse has experienced some of the value of being in this relationship.

Next comes the test! The protective part of your spouse says, "Really? You think this is a *good* person? Watch what happens when *this* button is pushed."

My guess is that your spouse knows which buttons to push. The key to passing the test is not to get defensive! If you do, your spouse points at your defensiveness as confirmation that they were right about you, reinforcing the belief that they have to leave if they're going to be happy. Do everything you can to stay calm.

For now, take a deep breath, exhale slowly, and remind yourself…

You can do this!

MARRIAGE RECALL

Mark what impact this topic is currently having on your marriage:

1	*2*	*3*	*4*	*5*

none   *needs reminder*   *needs repair*

Describe a similar experience you had relating with your spouse:

_____

_____

_____

What can you do differently using the skill outlined in this chapter?

_____

_____

_____

This week, apply your new skill and record your experience:

_____

_____

_____

_____

_____

_____

_____

_____

Make a new mark to track your progress. Don't give up!

1	*2*	*3*	*4*	*5*

none   *needs reminder*   *needs repair*

REMEMBER • **REPAIR** • RELOVE

WEEK 27 - PASSING THE TEST

"I've made some good changes. I've lost weight, I'm smiling and much more engaged. So why does my spouse seem *more* irritated with me?"

This catch-22 comes up often, and is confusing enough to merit explanation.

When you make healthy changes your spouse starts to experience the value of relating to you. Your spouse starts to see the "authentic you" they fell in love with. This experience is often met with resistance because they begin to feel emotions they didn't think they could or would feel again. This makes your spouse feel vulnerable, and it's scary. Actions are taken to reduce the fear. Your spouse begins to test! Buttons are pushed to get the "old you" back, so that they can continue to walk away with confidence.

The bad news is that your spouse knows which buttons to push. The good news is that you know which buttons will be pushed!

I used to spend a lot of time trying to figure out how to get the walk-away spouse to stop pushing buttons. This effort was mostly fruitless. A better use of your time is to *reprogram the button*, so that when it's pushed, your spouse gets something different than what is expected. When a negative response, like defensiveness, sarcasm, or anger is expected, and you give calm, confident, or playful instead, you pass the test with flying colors.

This creates a very disruptive thought process for your spouse. "What if I'm wrong? What if my spouse *is* capable of significant change, and these new behaviors are genuine and permanent?" If this is true it would be absurd for your spouse to walk away. But the changes need to be tested if your spouse is going to be able to trust them enough to reconcile. *Testing is a good thing.*

My conviction is that your spouse *wants you to pass* the test, if not completely, at least in part. You might be thinking, "You don't know my spouse!"

I grew up in Michigan, and by early December the ponds would start to freeze over. Every kid in the neighborhood knew what that meant—skating, sledding, snowmobiling, and hockey! But first we had to test the ice. We would get sturdy sticks and try to break through the ice. We would drop small rocks and then bigger rocks. Did we do this because we wanted the ice to break? No! We wanted to get out and enjoy the ice—but only if we had confidence it was going to hold.

You are working now to give your spouse that same confidence!

You can do this!

MARRIAGE RECALL

Mark what impact this topic is currently having on your marriage:

1	2	3	4	5

none   *needs reminder*   *needs repair*

Describe a similar experience you had relating with your spouse:

_____

_____

_____

What can you do differently using the skill outlined in this chapter?

_____

_____

_____

This week, apply your new skill and record your experience:

_____

_____

_____

_____

_____

_____

_____

_____

Make a new mark to track your progress. Don't give up!

1	2	3	4	5

none   *needs reminder*   *needs repair*

REMEMBER • **REPAIR** • RELOVE

WEEK 28 - RESPECT YOURSELF!

When a marriage is struggling, it's not unusual for people to feel down, discouraged and unmotivated. However, without a healthy dose of self-respect, you will send a mixed message to your spouse. It's as if you're saying, "Hey, I am a valuable, worthwhile person and you should treat me well. I'm not going to do it, *but I expect you to!*"

This isn't the way the world works. People are generally treated with about as much respect as they treat themselves. Think about those you deeply respect. How do they present themselves? They probably show appropriate levels of self-care. They value themselves by living physically, spiritually, emotionally, financially, socially, and intellectually healthy. They are not arrogant and self-centered. They have self-respect and they invite others to treat them in a similar fashion. I strongly encourage you to follow this model.

One of my clients, a wife and mother in a struggling marriage, was used to serving everyone else but didn't have a clue what *she* wanted. We talked about interests, hobbies, and dreams—but she came up empty. We finished our session without any goals identified.

A few weeks later, this same woman jumped out of an airplane. She had gone skydiving! I laughed so hard as she described her experience. Nearly sixty years old, afraid of heights, and because she didn't know what the altitude would do to her bladder, she stooped to wearing an adult diaper!

When we finished laughing, I asked what her husband thought of her wild stunt. She said his response was fascinating. He didn't know she had gone skydiving. Her sister grabbed her first thing in the morning and dragged her to the airfield. She saw her husband later that day, but before she could say a word he said, "What in the world have you been up to?" She didn't know exactly what he saw—a little bounce in her step, a twinkle in her eye—but whatever it was it got his attention. She knew she felt very different, and obviously he saw a difference in her, too.

Do you know what puts a bounce in your step? If you do, I hope you spend time pursuing it. If you don't, find out, then take some steps to pursue it! You may be amazed how you respond, and how others respond to you.

You can do this!

MARRIAGE RECALL

Mark what impact this topic is currently having on your marriage:

1	*2*	*3*	*4*	*5*

none   *needs reminder*   *needs repair*

Describe a similar experience you had relating with your spouse:

_____

_____

_____

What can you do differently using the skill outlined in this chapter?

_____

_____

_____

This week, apply your new skill and record your experience:

_____

_____

_____

_____

_____

_____

_____

Make a new mark to track your progress. Don't give up!

1	*2*	*3*	*4*	*5*

none   *needs reminder*   *needs repair*

REMEMBER · **REPAIR** · RELOVE

WEEK 29 - COMING ALIVE!

Self-care is critical as you work on a struggling relationship. It's essential to refuel in order to arrive at the destination of a healthy, thriving marriage.

This is important! Avoid the "spouse reaction filter." When you think of ways to improve your self-care, you're tempted to evaluate every choice you make based on the question, "How will my spouse react if I make this change?"

While I understand this is a good question, it is not the primary question!

You might be tempted to put things on your list that will make your spouse happy. For instance, you might consider going to the gym. Obviously this is a healthy choice. For some people going to the gym puts a bounce in their step, it gives them energy, and helps bring out the best in them. For others, going to the gym is drudgery, a task that drains energy and is filled with dread. However, some do it anyway to *please their spouse*.

If you're in the first group, have at it. But if you're in the second, find something else fast! You aren't going to sustain this activity for long, and no bounce will be added to your step!

The primary question is, "What makes *me* come alive?" John Eldredge, author of *Wild At Heart* writes, "Don't ask what the world needs. Ask 'what makes me come alive?' Because what the world needs is [people] who have come alive."

What puts a bounce in your step and draws out the best you can be? If you tap into this, it's not only sustainable but gives back more than you put in. It changes how you perceive yourself, and how you present yourself to others.

However, sometimes what makes you come alive brings conflict between you and your spouse. Then what? One of my clients talked with me about his love for motorcycles. He was so excited, by the end of the discussion I was ready to go buy one! Motorcycles were clearly part of his self-care. But he knew he couldn't buy one. When he and his wife got married, she read him the riot act about the dangers of riding a motorcycle. If he bought one now she would see it as vindictive. What should he do? We discussed the pros and cons, and he decided to go ahead and get a motorcycle.

We prepared for the push back, and it came. He assured his wife, to the best of his ability, that he was only doing what he needed to get on with his life. When he got his bike he put a huge bounce back in his step. Three months later his wife was getting *her* motorcycle license!

So, what puts a bounce in *your* step?

You can do this!

MARRIAGE RECALL

Mark what impact this topic is currently having on your marriage:

1	2	3	4	5

none   *needs reminder*   *needs repair*

Describe a similar experience you had relating with your spouse:

_____

_____

_____

What can you do differently using the skill outlined in this chapter?

_____

_____

_____

This week, apply your new skill and record your experience:

_____

_____

_____

_____

_____

_____

_____

_____

Make a new mark to track your progress. Don't give up!

1	2	3	4	5

none   *needs reminder*   *needs repair*

REMEMBER • **REPAIR** • RELOVE

WEEK 30 - THE OPPOSITE ATTRACTION

"What do I do if I get served with divorce papers?" This is a difficult question if you are the one trying to reconcile with your spouse.

Here are some thoughts that can help get you through this tough situation.

Remember, your spouse probably has a very clear expectation that you'll respond negatively. If your spouse gets what is expected, their belief will be reinforced. This convinces them they're doing the right thing. You want to give them something *completely different*.

There are two typical expectations.

First, your spouse expects you to ramp up your efforts to change their mind by begging, pleading, sending flowers, giving gifts, and offering promises to change. These probably haven't been very effective so far, but you might be tempted to try again.

Second, your spouse expects you to respond only when you absolutely have to. If you're required to respond within 30 days, your spouse expects to hear from you at the last minute on the 30th day.

Doing either of these rarely makes much progress. So what *should* you do?

Respond quickly—within 48 hours if possible—by opening up a friendly dialog. This means you're going to have to talk about what you don't want to talk about. I suggest something like, "I was thinking about how we're going to split up the assets. Obviously, I'm going to take my dad's hunting rifles, and you'll have your grandmother's armoire. But what are your thoughts about that painting we both like?" If your spouse is willing to engage, your mission is to listen, listen, and then listen some more.

You're not going to agree, or disagree, or argue. Your goal is to understand your spouse. If your spouse feels understood, your beginning to make progress.

Summarize your spouse's desires verbally, until it's clear you've understood them. Thank your spouse for sharing them with you. Tell your spouse you have a lot to think about and ask for time to digest the information.

I'm often asked, "Doesn't this just make it easier for my spouse to leave?" The short answer is "yes." But your spouse doesn't need your permission or your cooperation to walk away. What your spouse needs is a really good reason to stay!

You can do this!

MARRIAGE RECALL

Mark what impact this topic is currently having on your marriage:

1	*2*	*3*	*4*	*5*

none   *needs reminder*   *needs repair*

Describe a similar experience you had relating with your spouse:

_____

_____

_____

What can you do differently using the skill outlined in this chapter?

_____

_____

_____

This week, apply your new skill and record your experience:

_____

_____

_____

_____

_____

_____

_____

_____

Make a new mark to track your progress. Don't give up!

1	*2*	*3*	*4*	*5*

none   *needs reminder*   *needs repair*

REMEMBER • **REPAIR** • RELOVE

WEEK 31 - THE GOOD STUFF

When I meet with a spouse facing an unwanted divorce, I encourage them to believe in a turn-around. They tell me, "Oh, you don't know my spouse. When he makes up his mind—he'll *never* change. He wants a divorce and that's final. He's as stubborn as a mule!"

This always brings a smile to my face—and not the mean-spirited kind. I'm smiling because I disagree whole-heartedly with these statements. Here's why:

Isn't the person you described the same person who stood with you at a church altar, or before a justice of the peace—with a room full of witnesses—and said, "Until death do us part"? Was your spouse lying? Confused? Uncertain? Not according to the description given above. "When he makes up his mind—he'll *never* change. He's as stubborn as a mule!"

Your spouse knows what they want and sticks with it. And now, just a few short years later, your spouse is saying the exact opposite of what was said at the altar.

You see my point. Your spouse is capable of significant changes in position on very important topics. Another turn-around could be just around the corner!

Your spouse does not want a divorce! People dream of graduating, working in an exciting career, getting married, having children, getting divorced, buying their dream home, retiring and traveling around the world. Which one of the scenarios does *not fit* the good dreams of most people?

What your spouse wants is love, respect, friendship, intimacy, hope, forgiveness, trust, fun, laughter, security—and other fine desires. The problem is that your spouse no longer believes these things are possible in the marriage, so in order to be happy— your spouse must leave.

Your mission, if you choose to accept it, is to invite your spouse to experience more of the good things that are desired. Starting now!

What can you do today to let your spouse experience more of the good stuff? Offer a smile, a kind word, a gentle touch, a listening ear, playfulness, or a small act of service.

Start small. Be consistent.

And while you're at it, challenge your *own* thinking. If you expect your spouse to be unmovable, you could diminish your impact. Choose to fulfill your dream by thinking, "My spouse is so stubborn, once he gets a taste of the good stuff I'm dishing out—he'll never walk away!!"

Doesn't that feel better?

You can do this!

MARRIAGE RECALL

Mark what impact this topic is currently having on your marriage:

1	2	3	4	5
none		*needs reminder*		*needs repair*

Describe a similar experience you had relating with your spouse:

_____

_____

_____

What can you do differently using the skill outlined in this chapter?

_____

_____

_____

This week, apply your new skill and record your experience:

_____

_____

_____

_____

_____

_____

_____

_____

Make a new mark to track your progress. Don't give up!

1	2	3	4	5
none		*needs reminder*		*needs repair*

REMEMBER • **REPAIR** • RELOVE

WEEK 32 - THE HUNT

"T-Rex doesn't want to be fed, he wants to hunt!" Dr. Alan Grant made this comment in the movie *Jurassic Park* when he saw the goat presented as a meal to the mighty Tyrannosaurus Rex.

What does this have to do with marriage reconciliation? Many of my clients discover that their spouse wants to *hunt* instead of being *hand-fed*. If the process of reconciliation is too easy your spouse may not be able to embrace your value.

I understand the temptation to try to make it as easy as possible for your spouse to choose reconciliation. Spouses are sometimes desperate to do everything they can to save their marriages. However, if this process is taken too far it could work against you.

Imagine that you are on the Spouse Auction Block, and the auctioneer says, "Let's start the bidding at $500,000." You're afraid that your spouse won't pay that much, so you lean over to the auctioneer and whisper, "How about starting the bid at $50?"

Your spouse recognizes a great deal and pays the $50! So what's the problem? The problem is that they didn't have to realize your true value. Your spouse will then be tempted to treat you like a $50 spouse, which neither of you is going to enjoy for very long.

This is why it's important to focus on the value. As your spouse gets more of the good stuff—kind words, smiles, acts of service, playfulness, attentive listening, physical affection—they will be more likely to pay the price that reflects your value.

Clients who are wildly successful aren't satisfied with simply avoiding divorce. Wildly successful clients build marriages where each spouse is profoundly aware of the value, and willingly pays the price to be a partner.

Don't make it too easy. *T-Rex wants to hunt!*

You can do this!

MARRIAGE RECALL

Mark what impact this topic is currently having on your marriage:

1	2	3	4	5

none   *needs reminder*   *needs repair*

Describe a similar experience you had relating with your spouse:

_____

_____

_____

What can you do differently using the skill outlined in this chapter?

_____

_____

_____

This week, apply your new skill and record your experience:

_____

_____

_____

_____

_____

_____

_____

_____

Make a new mark to track your progress. Don't give up!

1	2	3	4	5

none   *needs reminder*   *needs repair*

REMEMBER • **REPAIR** • RELOVE

WEEK 33 - DISQUALIFIERS

The first time I met Michele Weiner-Davis, author of *Divorce Busting*, was at her advanced workshop for professionals. We learned theories and techniques, and had the opportunity to practice them. I remember when Michele told her story, giving us an honored glance into the pain that motivates her to excel at saving marriages.

Then she asked the group about *our* stories and what drives us to do this work. We heard story after painful story of people who had experienced divorce—their parents' or their own. As I listened, I felt disqualified. I didn't deserve to be in that sacred place, with these good and honest people. I cheated. I hadn't paid the price.

My childhood family was unbroken. My parents were faithful to each other to the end. My mom, a registered nurse, cared for my dad in our home during the final weeks of his life. I saw love in action, day in and day out. My family is still unbroken. My wife, Jan, and I have been happily married for many years. We've certainly had our struggles, but I haven't personally experienced the pain of divorce.

Michele picked up on my apologetic tone, and would have none of it! She celebrated my story as much as any, and she wouldn't allow me to disqualify myself.

Healing begins with the strengths that an individual brings to the table, rather than wasting time bemoaning shortcomings. If I was going to be an effective coach, I had to learn to accept my strengths and work from them.

In the battle to restore your marriage, what strengths do you bring? To be effective, accept your strengths, and learn to make them work for you! If you have a great sense of humor, do you invite your spouse to laugh with you? If you're kind, does your spouse get to enjoy your kindness? When and how?

On the flip side, what ways do you disqualify yourself from being effective in your marriage? "I don't make enough money." "I'm not pretty enough." "I'm overweight." STOP IT! You can't hate yourself into loving yourself. Don't waste time bemoaning your shortcomings. Accept your strengths and work from them!

I've seen many courageous clients walk through this battle unyielding in their desire and commitment to live out of their strength. This is not arrogance or false bravado. This is *authentic* living!

You can do this!

MARRIAGE RECALL

Mark what impact this topic is currently having on your marriage:

1	2	3	4	5

none   *needs reminder*   *needs repair*

Describe a similar experience you had relating with your spouse:

_____

_____

_____

What can you do differently using the skill outlined in this chapter?

_____

_____

_____

This week, apply your new skill and record your experience:

_____

_____

_____

_____

_____

_____

_____

Make a new mark to track your progress. Don't give up!

1	2	3	4	5

none   *needs reminder*   *needs repair*

REMEMBER • **REPAIR** • RELOVE

WEEK 34 - GETTING PAID

~~~~~~

When was the last time you said to your employer, "I have worked hard and produced very solid results, but I don't want you to pay me!" Of course, the answer is "never." Why would you do such a thing?

Yet, I know couples that have taken this very approach when it comes to rebuilding trust.

I worked with a reconciling couple after the husband had an affair. I asked the wife how her husband could win back her trust. She said, "If he would let me look at his cell phone whenever I want, that would be a big help."

This was the same phone he used to communicate with the "other woman." The husband understood and agreed, and for the first few weeks he complied. At about week four the wife was frustrated because he stopped giving her access. His comment was, "She should trust me by now."

I asked him, "Are you ashamed of something on your phone?" (This is the closest I have ever come to getting punched by a client!) He was indignant, and told me that I was just fueling his wife's mistrust. He stood up to leave.

"Whoa, slow down big fella. I believe you." He stopped. I really did believe him otherwise I probably wouldn't have asked the question.

"You've done the work, I just want you to get paid! If she doesn't get to see the phone, you don't get paid." He was a very good businessman, and the analogy of getting paid landed with him.

We worked together for several months. From that point on, when he came home from work he placed his phone on the counter. During this time his wife picked up the phone only once—but she saw it on the counter every single day. Each time she experienced this humble, transparent act; another deposit was made in his trust account.

Are you getting paid for the good work that *you're doing*? Don't let stubbornness ruin your chance at success. Evaluate your stance. Keep doing the work, investing in the best outcome.

Don't punish yourself by holding back. Transparency builds trust and that is the best payment toward a restored marriage.

You can do this!

MARRIAGE RECALL

Mark what impact this topic is currently having on your marriage:

1	2	3	4	5

none   *needs reminder*   *needs repair*

Describe a similar experience you had relating with your spouse:

_____

_____

_____

What can you do differently using the skill outlined in this chapter?

_____

_____

_____

This week, apply your new skill and record your experience:

_____

_____

_____

_____

_____

_____

_____

Make a new mark to track your progress. Don't give up!

1	2	3	4	5

none   *needs reminder*   *needs repair*

REMEMBER • **REPAIR** • RELOVE

WEEK 35 - WRONG FOOT

In my work with distressed couples, I have the privilege of working with some good people who are highly motivated. Two general categories define people in this situation—the dissatisfied spouse and the spouse who wants to reconcile. The dissatisfied spouse no longer values the marriage. Most of my work is with the spouse who wants to reconcile and believes the marriage is worth the battle.

But this time I'm writing for the spouse who *wants to walk-away*.

Why? Many times the client who initially was the walk-away spouse has inspired me. The spouse who said, "I love you but I'm not *in love* with you." This was the spouse who checked out the greener grass, who wanted to pursue a relationship with another partner, to be free from the arguments—to enjoy the *peace-filled single life*.

So what happened? In short, this was the spouse who "won." They convinced their spouse that the marriage was over, that they were never coming back. The reconciling spouse finally had the nerve to believe them and pursue their own happiness. Now the shoe is on the other foot!

I've asked these clients, "If you could go back 6 months or a year and talk to yourself, what advice would you give to avoid this heartache?" Here are some of the best comments:

"You're not as irreplaceable as you think! My spouse told me I couldn't leave because we were soul mates, I'm irreplaceable, and my spouse couldn't love someone else with the same romantic passion we had! The truth is now I'm the one feeling replaced and discarded—and it hurts!"

"Don't believe it when your spouse says, 'I'll wait as long as it takes!' As the leaving spouse I felt in control, indestructible, believing the safety net was in place so I could take risks without worrying about the consequences. If the relationship with the other partner doesn't work out, 'I can always go back to my spouse.' Well, no, actually, you can't. It turns out the promise that they would wait 'as long as it takes!' has an expiration date." Who knew?!

"The person you are pursuing knows that you are willing to betray a loved one! How long do you think it will be before this impacts your current relationship? Often the new partner will become overly attached and needy, because you've demonstrated that you're willing to hurt people deeply. Or they will decide to 'do unto you before you do unto them.'" Either way, these relationships have a very high failure rate.

Dear dissatisfied spouse, fast forward a year and imagine things have turned out like one of these stories shared by my experienced clients. If you could come back to now, what would you tell yourself? Are you willing to listen to the *older, wiser you?* I hope so!

You can do this!

MARRIAGE RECALL

Mark what impact this topic is currently having on your marriage:

1	2	3	4	5

none *needs reminder* *needs repair*

Describe a similar experience you had relating with your spouse:

_____

_____

_____

What can you do differently using the skill outlined in this chapter?

_____

_____

_____

This week, apply your new skill and record your experience:

_____

_____

_____

_____

_____

_____

_____

Make a new mark to track your progress. Don't give up!

1	2	3	4	5

none *needs reminder* *needs repair*

REMEMBER • **REPAIR** • RELOVE

WEEK 36 - THOSE WE DO NOT SPEAK OF

In the movie *The Village*, directed by M. Night Shyamalan, dangerous creatures roam the woods. The settlers in the village have an anxious balance with them, an unspoken agreement that they will not go into the woods, and the creatures will not breach the boundaries of the village. These creatures are referred to as, "Those we do not speak of."

As a marriage counselor and coach I also have a group of creatures I refer to this way. If your spouse is in an affair, the affair partner is one such creature. I give very little time to the topic of the "other man" or the "other woman" for a few very good reasons.

First, they fall into the same category as the weather, the traffic, the economy, the war, and a favorite sports team. They have some impact on your life, but you have no control over them. Seriously, you have no control over your spouse, who *has* made promises to you!

You have even *less* control over the "other" who has promised you *nothing at all*.

Second, when your spouse is interacting with you, do you really want to invite your spouse to think about someone else? Early on the affair relationship is mostly fantasy—a dreamy place with no morning breath, PMS, bounced checks, stinky diapers, or flat tires. A time will come when talking about the other person is beneficial, but it's usually after the scales have tipped in your favor, when your spouse is interested again in building an amazing marriage with you.

Third, while it is tempting to find faults in the other person, you don't want your spouse to return to you because the affair partner is *lacking*. Your spouse may be tempted to just continue looking elsewhere. I want your spouse to return to your marriage because you have the qualities your spouse is looking for, not because their affair partner has shortcomings.

I've cut off many discussions with clients who want to waste too much time talking about "those we do not speak of." Instead, I encourage you to spend your time getting down to the real business at hand—revealing the best you so your spouse realizes *you* are the right choice!

Now that's something to talk about!

You can do this!

MARRIAGE RECALL

Mark what impact this topic is currently having on your marriage:

1	2	3	4	5

none   *needs reminder*   *needs repair*

Describe a similar experience you had relating with your spouse:

_____

_____

_____

What can you do differently using the skill outlined in this chapter?

_____

_____

_____

This week, apply your new skill and record your experience:

_____

_____

_____

_____

_____

_____

_____

Make a new mark to track your progress. Don't give up!

1	2	3	4	5

none   *needs reminder*   *needs repair*

REMEMBER • **REPAIR** • RELOVE

WEEK 37 - DON'T SAY IT, DO IT!

"Let me get this straight," my client said. "My husband is walking away from our marriage because he doesn't believe I love him, and you want me to *stop saying* 'I love you'?"

Yes, you heard me right!

When a spouse decides to walk away from their marriage, they've been collecting data for a while. Months or even years before the bomb is dropped the hypothesis is formulated. "I'm not happy, and, hey, my spouse has been here this whole time. My spouse *must* be the cause of my unhappiness!" Once this speculation starts the data is gathered, sorted, and stored. The unsuspecting spouse continues to provide more and more evidence through their annoying habits, irritable moods, and selfish moments. The verdict? You don't love me, so I'm leaving.

When I suggest that you stop saying "I love you," I'm not suggesting you adopt a mean-spirited, "I'll show you, you louse" kind of an attitude. No, you *do* need to be loving, just stop saying it—for now.

The first reason is that most dissatisfied spouses will respond to "I love you" with their list of grievances (formulated from the data mentioned above). "NO, you don't! Because if you loved me, you would've said X, stopped doing Y, and remembered to do Z!" Stop inviting your spouse to run through their list. You won't come away from their internal dialog in a good light.

The second reason is that your "I love you" can often feel manipulative. Your spouse reacts to this felt manipulation with, "You don't love me, you just want to hear me say that I love you!" Again, the favorable light doesn't shine upon you.

Instead, offer specific affirmations, such as, "I love how patient you are with the kids," or "You are so quick to see the positive side of people, I love that." These affirmations should be offered without the expectation of a returned compliment. Start here and you will communicate love more genuinely than with a generic, pressure-filled, "I love you."

Take your time and continue to affirm your love in meaningful ways that helps your spouse replace their list of grievances with positive interactions.

When it becomes clear that progress has been made, such as your spouse moves back home or divorce papers are withdrawn, it may be time to say those three simple words again.

You can do this!

MARRIAGE RECALL

Mark what impact this topic is currently having on your marriage:

1	2	3	4	5

none   *needs reminder*   *needs repair*

Describe a similar experience you had relating with your spouse:

_____

_____

_____

What can you do differently using the skill outlined in this chapter?

_____

_____

_____

This week, apply your new skill and record your experience:

_____

_____

_____

_____

_____

_____

_____

Make a new mark to track your progress. Don't give up!

1	2	3	4	5

none   *needs reminder*   *needs repair*

REMEMBER • **REPAIR** • RELOVE

WEEK 38 - ASK ME AGAIN!

He was angry, but I just couldn't let it go. "I am so tired of answering the same questions over and over and over again," he said. "She doesn't believe my answers about the affair anyway, so why should I keep trying?"

"Were you telling her the truth just now?" I pushed. "Yes!" he answered. I pushed again, "Are you sure?" "Yes, yes I'm sure!" he said louder. One last verbal shove, "Really?" He looked at me fiercely.

"Are you angry with me?" I asked. "What do you think?" he admitted and then looked down. "I think I'd be angry, too," I replied.

How often should questions about an affair be asked? How many weeks or months need to go by until it can finally be put to rest?

If you have betrayed your spouse with an emotional or sexual affair, here's the challenge. The burden lies on your shoulders to win back your spouse's trust. The struggle is twofold.

First, it can feel punitive. You might feel the shame of the affair again each time the conversation happens. Second, there's no relief in sight. How do you measure progress when the same question needs to be answered that was answered last week, or last month, or six months ago?

It may seem otherwise, but I doubt your goodhearted spouse finds deep pleasure watching you squirm. But your spouse might need to see your remorse, your repentance—your godly grief. The fact that the questions bother you helps your spouse believe that your betrayal does not define you. This is not who you are—but it *is* something you have done.

How do you measure progress? Be consistent. It's imperative that you tell the truth; beginning as soon as you can, then answer the question whenever asked. "We were at the Hilton." "It was the Hilton." "We met at the Hilton." Your spouse gains comfort hearing answers that don't waver or change, and will eventually lead to the question not needing to be asked again.

What if you had a magic number? Let's say that numbet is 712. Once you have consistently answered the same question 712 times you never have to answer it again. It is an irrationally high number, but you can trust it. How would this affect your response? I suspect it would be different, hopefully even non-defensive.

"Come on, ask me again. I know you're tired, but it's for your own good. We're on question number 432! Just ask me a few more times tonight, OK?"

This scenario sounds crazy! However, it's your openness to the questions and consistency of your answers that helps bring healing to you and your spouse.

You can do this!

MARRIAGE RECALL

Mark what impact this topic is currently having on your marriage:

1	2	3	4	5

none   *needs reminder*   *needs repair*

Describe a similar experience you had relating with your spouse:

_____

_____

_____

What can you do differently using the skill outlined in this chapter?

_____

_____

_____

This week, apply your new skill and record your experience:

_____

_____

_____

_____

_____

_____

_____

Make a new mark to track your progress. Don't give up!

1	2	3	4	5

none   *needs reminder*   *needs repair*

REMEMBER • **REPAIR** • RELOVE

WEEK 39 - YAY FOR THE 10K!

I've been running for a while now, something I never thought I'd do. I even ran the Bolder Boulder, a popular 10K here in Colorado.

When I completed the run, several of my "fitness oriented" friends and family commented that I should try a half-marathon! What had I gotten myself into?! I felt a bit overwhelmed.

This is how many spouses react when they're seeing progress in their marriage reconciliation. They're taking better care of themselves physically, spiritually, and emotionally; they're experiencing easier conversations, more laughter, and increased affection in their relationship.

Then suddenly they burst like an unstoppable geyser, "So, are we going to work on this marriage or what? Are you IN or are you OUT? I'm sick and tired of being in limbo!"

I'm afraid this feels like you just tried to sign your spouse up for a half-marathon when they barely finished a 10K! Your spouse may end up running, just not in the direction you expected!

It would be great to know that your spouse is ready to take some risks that will move your relationship forward. However, if it feels overwhelming, your spouse might use the pressure as evidence that the marriage is never going to work. Your effort to push your spouse toward the next level has actually stirred resistance.

Oops!

You want to strike while the iron is hot, motivate the next step, and get this puppy going. However, if your spouse doesn't get to celebrate recent accomplishments, training for the half-marathon will be even more difficult—if not out of the question.

No, no, and again, no! Don't rush this. Stay patient. When you feel the pressure building, take a deep breath, hold it, exhale slowly—and then repeat this exercise again. Celebrate the progress you and your spouse have made and remember that things are moving in the right direction.

I hope you genuinely celebration the 10K! Then let your spouse bring up the half-marathon when the time is right.

You can do this!

MARRIAGE RECALL

Mark what impact this topic is currently having on your marriage:

1	2	3	4	5

none   *needs reminder*   *needs repair*

Describe a similar experience you had relating with your spouse:

_____

_____

_____

What can you do differently using the skill outlined in this chapter?

_____

_____

_____

This week, apply your new skill and record your experience:

_____

_____

_____

_____

_____

_____

_____

Make a new mark to track your progress. Don't give up!

1	2	3	4	5

none   *needs reminder*   *needs repair*

REMEMBER • **REPAIR** • RELOVE

WEEK 40 - DON'T GIVE UP

Clients often come to me in a fairly panicked state and ask, "So, what are my chances of reconciling this marriage?"

I'm not a bookie, I can't give odds on reconciliation—but I can give you two exceptional reasons for hope.

First, you're headed in the right direction. What would you say the chance is that your spouse would spontaneously return to a deeply unsatisfying marriage—one where you made no effort to change? 10% maybe?

But you've changed how you're relating; you're focused on the value. You've seen some small but clearly positive results. If the chances are now 30%, you're still on the uphill climb, but you're three times more likely to succeed than you were when you started!

Second, this is a worthy battle. In Victor Frankl's book, *Man's Search for Meaning*, he writes that we don't seek a "tensionless state" where we are carefree and coasting along. We long for, and are most alive, when we engage in a battle that is worthy of us. Frankl was a psychiatrist that survived the Auschwitz death camp in World War II. He understood the worthy battle of staying alive against all odds.

On June 6, 1944, Allied Troops invaded Normandy, France. 100,000 soldiers raced headlong through minefields, while heavy artillery fired against them. They had no guarantee of success. They had one driving force—this is a battle that must be fought! They pursued their noble cause willingly and courageously.

Your marriage is a noble cause. If you succeed many lives will be positively impacted. *Don't give up.*

I have worked with clients whose spouses wouldn't reconcile. Did they fail? Most of them adamantly declare that they did *not* fail. They fought the noble fight, they grew into a person who is more alive and vibrant than they ever imagined. And many have told me, in spite of the divorce, they are proud of the work they've done. It helped them move forward with no regrets because they fought valiantly.

If you feel like giving up, it's understandable. Take a break and renew your strength, assessing wisely what has had positive impact, then return to the battle of loving incredibly well. *Leave no regrets.*

You can do this!

MARRIAGE RECALL

Mark what impact this topic is currently having on your marriage:

1	2	3	4	5

none   *needs reminder*   *needs repair*

Describe a similar experience you had relating with your spouse:

_____

_____

_____

What can you do differently using the skill outlined in this chapter?

_____

_____

_____

This week, apply your new skill and record your experience:

_____

_____

_____

_____

_____

_____

_____

_____

Make a new mark to track your progress. Don't give up!

1	2	3	4	5

none   *needs reminder*   *needs repair*

REMEMBER • **REPAIR** • RELOVE

WEEK 41 - BETWEEN MAGICAL AND MISERABLE

Celebrations can be a challenging time for distressed couples. All of the festivities during holidays or hubbub of family gatherings can make everything seem more intense. When things go well—life can feel magical. When things go poorly—life can feel miserable.

The truth is that most of life is lived somewhere *between* magical and miserable. You can actually thrive during seasons of celebration with some thoughtful preparation.

I can usually tell when one of my clients is on the magical/miserable rollercoaster. If I hear words like "always" or "never" along with descriptions like "horrible" or "awesome," it's an indication of extreme, black-and-white thinking. While a rollercoaster ride can be exhilarating, it can also be exhausting. Being exhausted can lead to big mistakes and bad choices.

Take a wiser approach so you can enjoy life's celebrations.

First, challenge black-and-white thinking. If you head into a situation expecting it "to be perfect!" you're looking for magical.

Instead, stating, "This should be fun," or "I'm looking forward to relaxing with good friends," allows you to be positive without pressuring yourself (or others) to make it magical.

If you think, "This is going to be terrible!" challenge your thought process. "I can get through this," or "Someday I'll look back at this and laugh," are alternative thoughts that can keep you (and others) from ending up miserable.

Second, focus on being patient. Your marriage didn't disintegrate overnight, and it won't heal that quickly, either. The rollercoaster wants to go fast and get immediate results. However, sustained growth takes time and it is always worth the wait. Adjust your trajectory toward small changes that are clearly positive, and then give it time. Changing your course three degrees might not seem significant, but after a couple of weeks or a few months, you'll find yourself in a much better place.

Enjoy life's celebrations. Choose to live somewhere between "magical" and "miserable"—balancing the rollercoaster ride with moderate and realistic emotions and expectations.

You can do this!

MARRIAGE RECALL

Mark what impact this topic is currently having on your marriage:

1	2	3	4	5

none   *needs reminder*   *needs repair*

Describe a similar experience you had relating with your spouse:

_____

_____

_____

What can you do differently using the skill outlined in this chapter?

_____

_____

_____

This week, apply your new skill and record your experience:

_____

_____

_____

_____

_____

_____

_____

_____

Make a new mark to track your progress. Don't give up!

1	2	3	4	5

none   *needs reminder*   *needs repair*

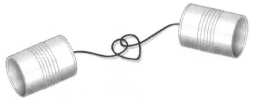

REMEMBER • **REPAIR** • RELOVE

WEEK 42 - OKAY, GIVE UP!

"Don't you ever tell someone to give up on their marriage?" I'm asked this question by those who are low on hope. They're looking for "permission" to give up. I understand the hurt and sorrow that are behind such a difficult question. However, I've seen too many amazing turnarounds when all seemed lost to declare that the battle is over. If you are out of gas, though, what can you do?

Let's say you decide it's over, and you give yourself permission to give up. How will you live differently tomorrow? Two responses are often shared.

The first response goes something like, "I'd buy that motorcycle I've been checking out," or "I'd finally go ahead and remodel the kitchen," or "I'd chase after my dream job to be a writer." In other words, "I've been putting a significant part of my life on hold, something that I would deeply enjoy, that would energize me and make me feel alive again." So I tell them, "Okay, give up!"

I'm not really giving up on the marriage. Pursuing your dreams doesn't preclude reconciliation. Think about it. What were you doing when you first won the heart of your spouse? Was your life on hold waiting for the right person to come along and make your life good? Probably not. You were enjoying fun activities and hobbies, like buying a motorcycle and pursuing your dream job. When your spouse became interested you were living your values. This type of authentic living is also the best chance to reconcile your marriage.

The second response raises all kinds of red flags. "I'd sign up for an online dating service," or "I'd pursue that office romance." This person is trying to make someone else responsible for their happiness. This comes from the belief that their spouse is just the *wrong person*. The solution, therefore, is to go out and find the *right person*. Problem solved! Except, what if you didn't pick the wrong person? What if *you* became the wrong person? What if the disappointments, hurts, frustrations, and fears that you experienced in your marriage drew out the worst in you? Sure, the excitement of a new relationship may bring out the best in you for a while. But if you didn't handle your disappointments well the first time, what makes you think you'll do better next time?

I'm not shaming anyone for running out of gas. I've worked with too many good, courageous people who have worked hard until, for various reasons, they were no longer able to carry on. I'm suggesting that you love and respect yourself enough to heal, to find a loving community of people where you can enjoy being you again. "Give up" the lie that someone "out there" is responsible for your happiness. Instead, "Give up" putting your life on hold and plan your next adventure.

Authentic living is healthy living—and it's *very attractive*.

You can do this!

MARRIAGE RECALL

Mark what impact this topic is currently having on your marriage:

1	*2*	*3*	*4*	*5*

none   *needs reminder*   *needs repair*

Describe a similar experience you had relating with your spouse:

_____

_____

_____

What can you do differently using the skill outlined in this chapter?

_____

_____

_____

This week, apply your new skill and record your experience:

_____

_____

_____

_____

_____

_____

_____

Make a new mark to track your progress. Don't give up!

1	*2*	*3*	*4*	*5*

none   *needs reminder*   *needs repair*

REMEMBER • **REPAIR** • RELOVE

WEEK 43 - DROP THE ROPE

When my clients are confronted with their spouse's unhappiness, I hear comments like, "My spouse tells me she's done trying to fix our marriage. Done trying!? I didn't even know we had a *problem*." And, "This is so unfair. I had no idea my husband was so unhappy, and now that I do, he won't even give me a *chance* to change."

The temptation is to try to pull your spouse back into the marriage. To be honest, sometimes this works. So if you had this kind of bomb dropped on you, it's okay to give this a try. However, if your spouse responds by becoming more adamant about being "done," stop what you're doing immediately and read on!

The decision to walk away from a marriage is rarely a quick, simple decision. A spouse has typically labored, even grieved, for weeks, months, or longer, trying to determine if leaving is a good decision. Most of their turmoil has been hidden from the unsuspecting spouse (See *How to Be Naked In Marriage*, page 95). Actually, once a spouse has decided to leave it's not unusual for arguments to dramatically decrease. Your spouse is no longer fighting the battles, and the marriage seems to be on a positive path. This makes the announcement that your spouse is leaving that much more confusing.

So if pulling your spouse back into the marriage makes things worse, what should you do?

Drop The Rope! Have you ever been in a tug-of-war, both sides with their heels dug in, pulling for all they're worth, straining for every foot of progress? What happens when one side drops the rope? Well, the other side falls down first, but then they stop pulling the rope. If your walk-away spouse is in tug-of-war mode, all the energy to relax and enjoy interacting with you is lost. Each time you challenge your spouse's reason for leaving, heels will dig in deeper. Then your spouse will repeat all the reasons for leaving and they become that much more *real*. Don't invite your spouse to *repeat the reasons* again.

So how does this look in real life? Begin with key phrases; the comments that make you want to attack. For example, if your spouse accuses you of neglect, instead of a defensive response, try, "I hate that you felt neglected." If your spouse explains that you're just too different, smile and agree—saying something like, "We *are* pretty different!" One of the hardest to hear is when your spouse admits that they just don't love you any more. *OUCH!* "I want you to be happy" is a good way to drop the rope on this comment, because it's true and it's non-argumentative.

I know it seems like you're accepting your spouse's reasons for leaving as valid. Don't worry about this. The real hope is that your spouse will have a positive experience interacting with you, because if that happens your spouse is drawing closer—without you pulling the rope!

You can do this!

MARRIAGE RECALL

Mark what impact this topic is currently having on your marriage:

1	2	3	4	5
none		*needs reminder*		*needs repair*

Describe a similar experience you had relating with your spouse:

_____

_____

_____

What can you do differently using the skill outlined in this chapter?

_____

_____

_____

This week, apply your new skill and record your experience:

_____

_____

_____

_____

_____

_____

_____

_____

Make a new mark to track your progress. Don't give up!

1	2	3	4	5
none		*needs reminder*		*needs repair*

REMEMBER • **REPAIR** • RELOVE

WEEK 44 - MOLEHILLS OUT OF MOUNTAINS

"I keep telling my spouse that these problems are fixable. They're certainly not bad enough to warrant destroying our marriage and family!" I hear these desperate words when the bomb has dropped that their spouse has decided to leave. They plead for their spouse to stop making mountains out of molehills.

I encourage my clients to do something very different: Stop making molehills out of mountains!

If you're trying to talk some sense into your spouse, you'll probably end up making matters worse. Here's why:

Who is the walk-away spouse? The walk-away spouse is often described as a kind, caring, fun, good-hearted, hard working, and intelligent person—words that describe a pretty solid, healthy adult. And this helps explain why you are motivated to save your marriage! Why then, would this healthy adult be so careless to harm their own marriage and family? You could conclude your spouse has good reasons— you just don't understand them yet.

The typical walk-away spouse has spent months or more agonizing over the decision to leave. When you make the argument that the problems are "no big deal" you tell your spouse, "I think you're stupid." This clearly isn't your intention, but it's often the message that is heard.

If your spouse is distressed enough to walk away, the problem is clearly not a molehill. It's a big problem that has become insurmountable. But let's say, for the moment, you're able to convince your spouse that the problem is *not that big of a deal*. It may feel like a success, but I fear you have created a bigger problem.

If you can't overcome this small problem in your marriage, what in the world will you do if a big problem hits! To a spouse who is aching for hope, this is the wrong solution.

So what can you do? Honor your mate's perspective that this really is a big problem, and that you're finally realizing it. You might fear that you're giving your spouse permission to divorce, but the reality is that your spouse doesn't need your permission!

Letting your spouse experience your genuine understanding, and even *remorse*, can have much more impact than debating the size of the problem.

You can do this!

MARRIAGE RECALL

Mark what impact this topic is currently having on your marriage:

1	2	3	4	5

none   *needs reminder*   *needs repair*

Describe a similar experience you had relating with your spouse:

_____

_____

_____

What can you do differently using the skill outlined in this chapter?

_____

_____

_____

This week, apply your new skill and record your experience:

_____

_____

_____

_____

_____

_____

_____

_____

Make a new mark to track your progress. Don't give up!

1	2	3	4	5

none   *needs reminder*   *needs repair*

REMEMBER • **REPAIR** • RELOVE

WEEK 45 - THE RED HERRING

When I work with a spouse fighting to save their marriage, I often ask, "What does your spouse find so intolerable that they would decide to walk away?" Simply put—*what are the complaints?* It's vital to understand the answer to this question.

A spouse decides to leave for various reasons. However, not all reasons are equal! Some carry more weight than others.

I don't know what matters to your spouse, but I do believe you can find clues to help you determine which complaints are *most* important.

The literary world offers a device called a *red herring*. A *red herring* is a detail or remark inserted into a discussion, either intentionally or unintentionally, that sidetracks the discussion. It's often used in mystery novels to lead a reader toward a false conclusion.

Red herrings also exist in the world of marriage reconciliation—mysteries that lead to false conclusions. You can use these two questions to help identify them.

Is the complaint about something new? A common response is "No, I was this way long before we met." This doesn't negate the complaint, but it might be a *red herring*. If you were disorganized, a football fanatic, or lacked initiative during courtship, something balanced what is now seen as "intolerable" behavior. Another piece is missing. Why didn't these behaviors bother your spouse then? Were you more fun, talkative, spontaneous, or thoughtful? If so, spend some time recapturing these positive qualities to see if they balance the false conclusion that you are intolerable.

Is the complaint resolvable? If your spouse is complaining about something that can't be changed, it's probably a *red herring*. "We used to travel at the drop of a hat when we first met." But you probably didn't have three kids, two dogs, and a mortgage then, either. "We biked everywhere during our courtship!" But if you just had knee surgery, you can't keep this up! If change isn't possible, acknowledge your spouse's disappointment without defensiveness. Then pursue activities that you *can* achieve, even if it doesn't initially seem to resolve your spouse's complaint.

When it comes to *red herrings*, I'm a fan of catch and release.

Identify the real issue (negative behavior or lack of activity), decide what adjustments are needed (add positive interactions, incorporate a new activity), then use your effort to pursue productive results—and throw that *red herring* overboard!

You can do this!

MARRIAGE RECALL

Mark what impact this topic is currently having on your marriage:

1	2	3	4	5

none　　　　　*needs reminder*　　　　*needs repair*

Describe a similar experience you had relating with your spouse:

_____

_____

_____

What can you do differently using the skill outlined in this chapter?

_____

_____

_____

This week, apply your new skill and record your experience:

_____

_____

_____

_____

_____

_____

_____

_____

Make a new mark to track your progress. Don't give up!

1	2	3	4	5

none　　　　　*needs reminder*　　　　*needs repair*

REMEMBER • **REPAIR** • RELOVE

WEEK 46 - OVERCOME THE ODDS

"My wife has a bunch of family and friends who encourage her to go through with the divorce. Even her counselor tells her to leave! How can I beat that!?"

When the battle to save your marriage seems stacked against you, it can be very discouraging. Here are some dos and don'ts that can help you overcome the odds:

Don't attack your spouse's allies. You might be thinking, "If I can just pry him away from those manipulative people!" Keep in mind, your spouse sees "those" people as allies. If you attack them, your spouse is likely to push back and defend them. The more energy your spouse uses to defend them, the more vested your spouse becomes in their position against you.

Find common ground. If her counselor has written a book, or a blog, read it! Look for something that you can genuinely embrace, and then learn to speak that language. If your spouse talks about setting boundaries, finding a voice, or codependent choices, learn what that means and understand your spouse's goals. Verbalize your support for healthy growth, and even show genuine admiration for the therapist's insights.

Don't recruit friends and family. It's tempting to recruit those who support reconciliation to go "talk some sense" into your spouse. They will naturally say what seems right to them. You don't want to orchestrate the alienation of your spouse's support network. Gently withdraw from talking about the marriage with them. This can be seen as loving and respectful when your spouse discovers it.

Applaud growth when you see it. I had a client who complained for years about her husband's procrastination. Her husband overcame his problem—when it came to *filing for divorce*! Instead of demeaning him, she was able to authentically affirm his growth in taking this difficult step. He appreciated her kind words, and began to see her as an ally who supported him.

Remember, you used to be your spouse's greatest ally—and you probably had more influence than anyone. You didn't attack support systems, condemn healthy actions, show disrespect, and ignore signs of growth. You became an ally by understanding dreams, showing interest, and by giving sincere affirmation and encouragement.

Don't waste your precious time attacking your spouse's allies, become one instead!

You can do this!

MARRIAGE RECALL

Mark what impact this topic is currently having on your marriage:

1	2	3	4	5

none   *needs reminder*   *needs repair*

Describe a similar experience you had relating with your spouse:

_____

_____

_____

What can you do differently using the skill outlined in this chapter?

_____

_____

_____

This week, apply your new skill and record your experience:

_____

_____

_____

_____

_____

_____

_____

Make a new mark to track your progress. Don't give up!

1	2	3	4	5

none   *needs reminder*   *needs repair*

REMEMBER • **REPAIR** • RELOVE

WEEK 47 - THAT IS THE QUESTION

"Do you still have feelings for her?" his betrayed wife asked. "Uh-oh, how do I answer? I've committed to be honest while we reconcile, but it can't help to confess to my wife that I miss my affair partner! Won't that hurt *more*?"

Many of my clients face this challenge successfully. I believe being transparent and honest is an important part of healing. Honesty helps answer two important questions; "Why did the affair happen?" and "How can an affair be prevented from happening again?"

It's tempting to label the cheating spouse as "bad" and the betrayed spouse as "innocent"—but these labels miss the point.

The cheating spouse is responsible for the betrayal. Whatever factors influenced the decision, it was ultimately this spouse's choice. But consider this with me: Why would an otherwise good, kind, loving person make such a horrendous choice?

I believe the affair met a *legitimate need*, but in an *illegitimate way*.

Adopting the "bad spouse" belief often disregards the legitimate need and increases the chance that the need will continue to go unmet, possibly repeating the pattern down the road. Do you really want to go through this again? I don't think so!

The question, "Do you still have feelings for the other person?" has an inherant flaw. It assumes that the affair partner generates the positive emotions. This unfortunate assumption leads the betrayed spouse to believe that they must become more like the affair partner. If they don't do this well enough the affair partner is waiting in the wings. However, the positive emotions *actually* come from the cheating spouse.

Ask this important question differently to get a more transparent answer. What desire (legitimate need) did the other person meet? Answers I often hear are:

- *I felt important* because he listened to me.
- *I felt attractive* because of the way she looked at me.
- He always did nice things for me and *I felt valued.*
- *I felt respected* when my opinion mattered.
- When I was upset he understood and *I felt validated.*
- She asked for my opinion, and *I felt useful.*

Do you recognize the legitimate needs?

These answers can motivate us to act, grow, and find ways to meet one another's legitimate needs in *legitimate ways.* Listen for the queues, and then become an expert at meeting them. When you become the legitimate resource for your spouse's needs to be met, it can bring profound joy to both of you.

You can do this!

MARRIAGE RECALL

Mark what impact this topic is currently having on your marriage:

1	2	3	4	5

none   *needs reminder*   *needs repair*

Describe a similar experience you had relating with your spouse:

_____

_____

_____

What can you do differently using the skill outlined in this chapter?

_____

_____

_____

This week, apply your new skill and record your experience:

_____

_____

_____

_____

_____

_____

_____

_____

Make a new mark to track your progress. Don't give up!

1	2	3	4	5

none   *needs reminder*   *needs repair*

SECTION THREE - RELOVE

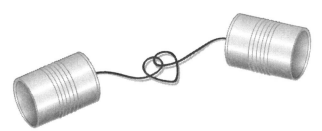

REMEMBER • REPAIR • **RELOVE**

REMEMBER • REPAIR • **RELOVE**

As a marriage counselor I've been part of many classes or events for couples, and I've found that they have a few things in common. Couples who attend often struggle with similar issues; before attending they felt they were the only ones struggling; *and* they've let those feelings drive them into isolation. However, most couples are pleasantly surprised to find the struggles are often common, and that they can learn to love their spouses *deeply* and *intentionally*.

The following chapters suggest resources to enhance your marriage that often go ignored until getting help is *critical*.

Don't wait! Have fun and build a strong connection as you:

- Read a really good book on marriage (*many* great books are available!).

- Enjoy a humorous or intimate look at married life by viewing various media online or via DVD.

- Take a personal survey to discover the different ways you relate to the world around you and more importantly, to one another.

- Visit various websites that are specifically designed to help you strengthen your marriage.

- Spend time together at an activity, class, or a marriage retreat to get away from the everyday—and focus on each other.

I often suggest a technique called Keep-Add-Remove. During our marriage my wife Jan and I have made regular choices to *keep* what we enjoy, *add* something new now and then, and *remove* what isn't working. This approach has given us a very *lively* marriage. If we can do this...

You can do this!

WEEK 48 - BOOKS TO READ

This list of books comes from our own library. We have been greatly energized, challenged, and encouraged by what we've learned about ourselves, each other, and the common experience of marriage that couples share. Have fun!

☑ 1. *The 5 Love Languages* by Gary Chapman
   The secret to showing love is learning the right love language.

☑ 2. *Sacred Marriage* by Gary Thomas
   Love your spouse with a stronger sense of purpose.

☑ 3. *Divorce Busting* by Michele Weiner-Davis
   A step-by-step approach to making your marriage loving again.

☑ 4. *For Women Only* and *For Men Only* by Shaunti Feldhahn
   Discover the truth your spouse wants you to know.

☑ 5. *How We Love* by Milan and Kay Yerkovich
   Discover your love style, enhance your marriage.

☑ 6. *The Sex-Starved Marriage* by Michele Weiner-Davis
   A couple's guide to boosting their marriage libido.

☑ 7. *Why Marriages Succeed or Fail* by John Gottman
   How you can make your love last with enlightening information.

☑ 8. *Love & Respect* by Emerson Eggerichs
   The love she most desires; the respect he desperately needs.

☑ 9. *Every Man's Marriage* by Stephen Arterburn and Fred Stoeker
   Establish mutual respect and sacrifice in your marriage.

☑ 10. *Every Woman's Marriage* by Shannon and Greg Ethridge
   Penetrating insights about how to nurture a dynamic marriage.

We have enjoyed many media presentations over the years that made a great point with humor and drama. They open us up emotionally, and teach a truth about marriage or relationships from a different point of view. Enjoy!*

☑ 1. Mark Gungor: *Laugh Your Way to a Better Marriage*
A DVD of fun antics that shows marriage tips and insights.

☑ 2. Tim Hawkins: *Full Range of Motion*
A DVD of energetic comedy that includes marriage topics.

☑ 3. Jeff Allen: *Happy Wife - Happy Life*
A DVD full of comedic new insights on family and marriage.

☑ 4. Anita Renfroe: *I'm Not High Maintenance - Just Low Tolerance*
Sassy comedy that is edgy and slightly offbeat about real life.

☑ 5. Dennis Prager Radio: *The Male/Female Hour*
A fun weekly radio broadcast on the challenge between the sexes.

☑ 6. Steve Arterburn: *New Life Live! Radio*
Daily radio broadcasts cover marriage, family, and personal topics.

☑ 7. Emerson Eggerichs: *Love and Respect Audio Books*
Deal with conflict quickly, easily and biblically with love and respect.

☑ 8. Rob Reiner's *The Story of Us* (R)
The highs, lows, and in-betweens of a couple at the crossroads.

☑ 9. Tyler Perry's *Why Did I Get Married?* (PG-13)
An intimate story about keeping a solid love relationship.

☑ 10. Alex and Stephen Kendrick's *Fireproof* (PG)
A firefighter faces a challenge in hopes to save his marriage.

Please use personal preference when viewing suggested movie titles.

These tools are sure to give you insight on how you relate, what styles you use, and why you choose certain ways to communicate. Understand your marriage—and enjoy your differences, and make sure to keep it fun. Take a peek!*

☑ 1. Discover Your Love Language
   5lovelanguages.com/profile

☑ 2. How We Love - Love Style Quiz
   howwelove.com/love-style-quiz

☑ 3. Trading Places Inventory
   lesandleslie.com/assessments/trading-places-inventory

☑ 4. Time Style Assessment
   lesandleslie.com/assessments/time-style

☑ 5. Marriage Building Exercises
   rd.com/advice/relationships/download-our-marriage-building-exercises

☑ 6. The Four Seasons of Marriage Quiz
   fourseasonsofmarriage.com/marriagequiz.asp

☑ 7. The Relate Questionnaire
   relate-institute.org/

☑ 8. The Relationship Center Survey Participation
   ritademaria.com

☑ 9. Prepare/Enrich - Facilitated Assessment
   prepare-enrich.com

☑ 10. Myers-Briggs Type Indicator - Online ($49.95)
   mbticomplete.com/en/index.aspx

*Surveys provide a snapshot and are not meant to define you or your marriage.

WEEK 51 - SITES TO SURF

These are just a few of the websites dedicated to helping marriages succeed. Filled with information, tips, resources, data, articles, blogs, videos, and more. Spend some of your online time investing in your marriage! Surf's up!

☑ 1. Divorcebusting.com - Michele Weiner-Davis
Coaching, resources, and open forums to save your marriage.

☑ 2. Newlife.com - Steve Arterburn
Christian counseling resources for marriage, sex addiction, and healing.

☑ 3. Growthrac.com - Jim and Sheri Mueller
Articles, newsletters, and blogs to build a better marriage.

☑ 4. Howwelove.com - Milan and Kay Yerkovich
Deep change is possible with resolution and understanding.

☑ 5. Daveramsey.com - Dave Ramsey
Get rid of debt, manage your money, spend and save wisely.

☑ 6. Understandingmen.com - Alison Armstrong
Insights, discoveries, and advice to understand men and women.

☑ 7. Shaunti.com - Shaunti Feldhahn
Research, insight, and hope for men, women, and relationships.

☑ 8. Familylife.com - Dennis and Barbara Rainey
Daily help and encouragement for a hopeful tomorrow.

☑ 9. Marriagesrestored.com - Ben and Anne Wilson
Redemption and restoration following infidelity in marriage.

☑ 10. Smartmarriages.com
The coalition for marriage, family, and couples education.

WEEK 52 - PLACES TO GO

There never seems to be enough time at home to focus on each other and our marriage—even though we're empty nesters. That's why we recommend getting away for time to grow, wander, and look into each others eyes. Go for it!*

☑ 1. New Life Marriage Weekend: newlife.com
   Rejuvenate, restore, or rescue your marriage for new hope.

☑ 2. Divorce Busting Personal Intensive: divorcebusting.com
   No marital problem is too severe to find seeds of hope and solutions.

☑ 3. Weekend To Remember: familylife.com
   Encouragement, hope, and practical tools to build your marriage.

☑ 4. Marriage Encounter: agme.org
   Sign off, get away, and examine your marriage in a realistic way.

☑ 5. Festival of Marriage: lifeway.com
   Your home can become the most powerful place on earth.

☑ 6. Worldwide Marriage Encounter: wwme.org
   Get away from everyday life and focus on each other.

☑ 7. Marriage Enrichment Retreat: ou.org
   Reinforce and strengthen your marital skills and tools.

☑ 8. Marriage Excitement Weekends: springfieldmfi.com/getaways.php
   Don't settle for "average," get the most out of your marriage.

☑ 9. Classes for Couples: hobbiesforcouples.com
   Create a life-long relationship sharing fun hobbies and interests.

☑ 10. Weekend Getaways: weekendgetawaysforcoupleshq.com
   Recreate your honeymoon excitement with a special time away.

Please use personal preference when selecting activity or retreat resources.

TIN CAN PHONES

People love nostalgia. It takes us back to a simpler time, a time when playfulness thrived, and words came easy. Our tin can phone graphic is a picture of such a time. A time in your marriage that we want to help you recall.

Over time communication breaks down. Knots get tied in the thread of conversation. Tin cans get dented and rusty in the wear and tear of everyday life.

Marriage Recall helps you recapture the early days of your relationship. Untie the knots and shine up the tin cans! Your work will help you remember and repair, until you recall all the reasons you fell in love, and can enjoy them intentionally!

If you have any feedback, stories to share, or resources to recommend please stay in touch:

www.chuckfallon.com
www.marriagerecall.com
info@chuckfallon.com

—

P.O. Box 150334
Lakewood, CO 80215

CONTACT CHUCK

Chuck Fallon, LPC, is a marriage counselor in private practice and a coach with Divorce Busting®, an internationally known organization founded by author Michele Weiner-Davis. Chuck serves as a Marriage Rescue and Every Man's Battle counselor with New Life Ministries at their conferences held annually throughout the United States. Chuck speaks at churches and groups on marriage and relationships from a spiritual and therapeutic perspective. He lives in Lakewood, Colorado, with his wife Jan and nearby their three grown sons.

In-office Appointments

Chuck is a licensed professional counselor in the State of Colorado. If you live in the Denver area, visit www.chuckfallon.com for information about in-office appointments at his Lakewood office.

Telephone Coaching

If you live outside of the Denver-area, contact Divorce Busting® at www.divorcebusting.com or 800-664-2435 to set up a telephone coaching session with Chuck.

Resources

For information about Chuck as a guest speaker at your church or event, for additional marriage resources, or to order copies of Marriage Recall, visit www.chuckfallon.com.

Phone: 720-299-5587 (Jan)
Email: info@chuckfallon.com
Web: www.chuckfallon.com

CPSIA information can be obtained at www.ICGtesting.com
Printed in the USA
LVOW13s1553230514

387112LV00001B/181/P